THE
SUBTLE CUES
—— OF ——
YOUR SOUL

THE SUBTLE CUES OF YOUR SOUL

Unique Ways to Sense Energy and Forge Connectedness

ALLIE V. BAKER

Tampa, Florida

The content associated with this book is the sole work and responsibility of the author. Gatekeeper Press had no involvement in the generation of this content.

THE SUBTLE CUES OF YOUR SOUL
Unique Ways to Sense Energy and Forge Connectedness

Published by Gatekeeper Press
7853 Gunn Hwy., Suite 209
Tampa, FL 33626
www.GatekeeperPress.com

Copyright © 2024 by Allie V. Baker

All rights reserved. Neither this book, nor any parts within it may be sold or reproduced in any form or by any electronic or mechanical means, including information storage and retrieval systems, without permission in writing from the author. The only exception is by a reviewer, who may quote short excerpts in a review.

Library of Congress Control Number: 2024948160

ISBN (paperback): 9781662950810
eISBN: 9781662950827

Like Morning Sunlight

Soul connection is like the morning sunlight
it feels Warm on the face
Gentle on the skin
and Familiar within the heart

It awakens to you slowly and with beautiful Grace
You need only to Welcome it
have Patience for its arrival
and Trust that you will recognize what is Yours to behold

MY GIFT TO YOU ALL

Following the death and physical departure of my mother, my loving her brought me to a place of solidified knowingness within myself. I was reawakened to the divine and eternal part of my deepest and most whole essence, the part of me that is reachable to her still, even past death and beyond earthly time. I slowly discovered the subtle cues and callings of my own soul. The ways in which energy and my essence communicate within one another. I began paying attention, and I have since witnessed many undeniable occurrences that have revealed to me how our energetic bonds with those whom we cherish most continue always. These bonds are strengthened by possessing a genuine belief of our loved one's continued existence in this world, beyond the death of the human body. Spirit continues to assist me with healing my heartbreak as I continue to witness her in all of the things that I do. Any time that I seek to find her near, she arrives for me.

I am most grateful for her staying close enough spirit-side for me to eventually come to learn that I truly can feel her near to me still, even through death and beyond loss. Our bond was one that was so extraordinary, and it is one that I am so fortunate to physically miss. It is my labor of love to share with you all the very same knowingness. For whomever it is that you miss . . . however it is that you lost them . . . no matter the time nor the space between then and now . . . I promise you that they still very much exist in this physical reality and alongside you. Their energy and essence is present when you call out for them, and they will arrive for you too if you can learn to pay attention to the subtle callings of your own soul.

The feelings, the sounds, the colors, the smells, the timing . . . how it all resonates within you and what it all means within your spirit is how you decipher your connectedness to your beloved in the present now. Fostering these connections can positively assist with the way that people grieve and ease their heartache to some degree. These connections can alter the way a person begins to heal as well as the ways that they can move forward through their loss and into the continuation of their life. The realization that our people still witness and experience our life along with us can be such a gift to our grief-ridden heart.

I believe that everyone could benefit from witnessing the truth of continued connectedness beyond bodily death. At some point in our lives, death will arrive for all of those that we love and ourselves. The only thing needed in order to begin one's quest towards continuing and fostering our bonds with our crossed-over beloved is some amount of dedicated time spent learning how one's own spirit speaks to them individually. How your spirit relays messages through you and to you is absolutely unique to you. It is all within you to find, pay attention to, and decode. If you choose to look within, you will uncover a great many wonderful and magic-like things arriving to you.

This handbook was written to share with you your own potential to uncover the continuing love with those whom you miss so very much. And so, with that, I hope you choose to take the time to unearth your own divinity. . . learn to breathe and how to calm your thinking, slow down your hurriedness and pause yourself for some consistent moments each day. Pray (in your own way) and trust that you will be enveloped in the love of your person as well as the many angels that help to light your way, for we are all loved beyond measure and supported without question.

Consistency and patience are both key when practicing returning to your truth and while learning the depths of yourself and the way that energy comes through to you best. Please remember that. Begin by believing in the possibility, for you must do so before you can be led to see! You will not get far in your spiritual journey if you doubt or question every single happenstance, deny synchronistic occurrences, or if you try to rationalize each sign that you receive. Choose to be faith-filled from the start. Specifically, be open and willing to believe that Spirit is very much a present and continuing piece of life. This is the way to becoming a witness to some amazing signs and synchronicities that will blow your mind and lift your heart. You are capable of finding your most cherished people again. Death is not the end of it all, folks . . . ! I promise you that.

With love and light,

~Allie

LOSS AND HEALING

One day, it will be you. If it hasn't already been. Death will arrive without warning and remove someone from their physical life in an instant. You will stand in time and space feeling lost and like you have just lost a love that cannot be replaced or replicated. This loss will appear to be the severing of a magnificent relationship. Your heart will shatter over the halting of a future, their death marking the end of an existence for that someone whom you love. It will be a massive loss, one that you did not choose to endure and one that time cannot return.

Grief will show up, feeling like heartbreak that will be pure torture. The world will seem to hold no air for you to breathe. It will look and feel like the end of a bond that was uniquely shared between the two of you and was unlike any other in your lifetime. Death seems to be the imposed completion of their loving support, and all because of the finality of their human life.

That is, it may seem to be this way until you come into yourself. Until you learn that the body only houses the soul. Until you trust that you can be forever bonded with your beloved. Until you allot time for practicing silence, observing what your "self" shows you, and accept opening up again to your knowingness of divinity.

Then, you will see.

The Essence of You

Another day is almost gone away
Previously I had found those words painful to say
When the sun would set it would feel like leaving you behind
in my yesterday and possibly further out of my mind
That is, until I found you within my Today
when Love and Light seemed to guide my way
In spirit and in soul you arrive
You have shown me that death is not a final goodbye
I rejoice in all that I now know to be true
As I bask in the love of the essence of you

OUR HEART'S ENERGY

Finding your way . . .

Unique and entirely personal to you, there comes a time that is life-altering on an emotional level you've not yet experienced in your life. A loss arrives, creating massive growth and perpetually changing everything at speeds that feel excruciating to you. These exceptionally impactful moments cause angst and great questioning and ultimately lead you into the person you were to become from such enormously challenging events.

In my case, the enlightenment and deepening of my spirituality and the coming into my knowing of eternal connection between my soul and all of the Universe came with the departure of my mother from this physical realm. With her death, I became altered. A shell of what I had known myself to be the day before. That immediate and unexpected event catapulted me towards my greatest capacity of growth. Time has never again stood so incredibly still while simultaneously whizzing by. My heart shattered, and I felt my spirit rupture instantly when I found out that she had died. Time, or what I could grasp of it, was a confusing spiral of nausea-producing waves. Functioning was merely an automatic repetition of the routines I had done over and over again. I could not accomplish things that were outside of those routines; they seemed to be foreign in nature, actions that I could not dissect or understand in any way. I did no thinking that I could decipher, as thought itself felt unmanageable, unreachable, and scary, and language looked like jumbled squiggles on a page, almost as though I was a tourist in a country foreign to my own. Words mumbled together as I'd watch people's lips move, but my ears did not hear the words that they spoke.

At least, I did not hear them in a way that I could understand. That was my grief in its earliest forms.

It was a time of loss that sent me into a fog that made it seem as though darkness clouded all of what I had previously thought to be my life. It all changed, all in one instant, with two small words spoken. In that brief moment, I had recognized that I was now void of the physical presence that was my mother. I was in my vehicle, and as I continued driving, I recall telling myself out loud, over and over, that my mother had died in hopes of beginning to process for myself what I knew was then to forever be my reality. In the following hours and days, I was thrust into all the considerations of what could have gone wrong, what might have happened, and how many ways I could play her dying out in my mind. So many unknowns made things feel so open-ended. No chance for goodbyes were afforded. As with any unknown, changes can be hard to swallow, and this one was unlike any I'd been thrust into before.

Years later, as I sit writing this, I see much of what I was to learn from such a profound loss in my life. I recognize how the timing was pivotal in ensuring I would be afforded enough time to learn my whys and to have enough earthside time to share the messages that I know that I am to be the sharer of. I understand now what service I am called to provide, and I do so with an eager heart and a genuine care for any tenderhearted person experiencing or having had experienced a life-altering loss. Coming to realize the dharma that her loss carries for me is relieving. It brings about feelings that make me understand that it was all required to take place the way in which it did in order for me to step into my own light. It reinstates to me once again that we are all here to learn and evolve, and in order to learn, we must grow through our experiences regarding love, service, suffering, living to our highest potential, extending trust to our Source, honoring our divinity, and to recalling our truths.

I am proud to carry the hopeful task of sharing the concept of fostering continued connections with our beloved people beyond their physical death with a world that needs to know its truth. With goals of mending shattered hearts and opening some eyes to the magic that is Spirit and all of the divine, I set out to share with you what I know, what I've been shown, and what kind of experiences you too are capable of having with your most cherished beings. Practice listening within and learning for yourself how to trust your own essence, listen with your intuition, and utilize the light of Source (God, Allah, Buddha, Universe, Creation . . . the name you use matters not) to heal and mend your own grieving heart. *Anyone* can begin to recognize the connections that eternally remain and the bonds that continue forever with the people that we love most. Everything is love, and everything is a frequency of energy.

I feel exceedingly blessed to have been gifted every sign and synchronic experience that I have witnessed. I am always grateful to observe these gifts, and I give thanks with each that I receive. Not one day passes when I do not feel massive gratitude for continuing to know my mother's energy and for having learned what her essence feels like around me now. Her soul in spirit is vibrant and lovely. The many prayers I have said have led me to a place of peace, knowing, and, ultimately, to reclaiming our love eternal.

So, it is with love that I share that I have arrived at knowings of divine truth, and you can too, if you are willing to do the work of opening your heart and leveling up your energies to become nearer to the plane that your beloved's energy now exists on. Meeting your loved one in the middle is easier than them having to slow their vibrations down to match your frequencies. It all takes practice, and this guidebook will suggest some of the ways that you can take time with yourself in order to learn just how to do that uniquely for you.

HER CHILDHOOD

My mother was raised Catholic in a family of five children back in the 1950s. Her sister Linda passed away from cancer at nine years of age. My mother was three years old at the time and was the youngest of the family. I recall her telling me of her only knowing of her sister's illness and how cancer and Linda's death impacted their family as a whole. Throughout my growing up, my Nana was someone that I was extremely close to. We spent considerable time together. She was wonderful and loving, and of course, she always carried the burden of losing a child, as any bereaved mother would. In her earlier years of adult life after the death of her second-oldest child, she had told my mother that, when Linda had passed, in the moments of her finality, she had spoken of the light that she had seen. Linda had told my Nana that God was real and that she wasn't afraid of death or her exit from this earth. This was a beautiful gift of comfort that couldn't have been appreciated by Nana in such a moment of sorrow.

The grief that my Nana experienced in the loss of her beloved daughter was numbing to her spirit. It made her question her faith and had her very angry with God. As with any bereaved parent, the pain was something that she carried always; it was something that changed her heart and altered her joy forever. She felt numb and depressed, and those feelings revisited her throughout her entire life. Certainly, losing a child was the worst torture anyone could endure.

The vastness of her continued grief did not allow for a peaceful calm to be found anywhere within her heart space, and therefore, she never got the chance to recognize the parts of her little girl that were still around her even after she had physically died. My Nana never believed in the possibility of fostering a continued connection with her Linda, because people simply did not consider such things back in those days. She wasn't aware of the bond that remained even though she could no longer see her precious child. Sure, parts of my Nana's spirit healed to some degree with time, and her grief, although ever present, became more integrated into her life as it moved forward . . . but their family's personal religious ideas of what was to be accepted and recognized as legitimate as far as life after death was concerned did not allow for any consideration of what might have been feasible to believe as far as continued connectedness was concerned. Heaven and Hell were spoken of as their truth, but no focus was placed on spirit and soul being able to forge continuing bonds past the final breath of someone they loved.

Things have changed so much from those years back when my mother was young. Religion would not have guided my Nana back to the knowingness of her young daughter's continued presence. Perhaps if spirituality was more openly shared back then, perhaps if the afterlife wasn't thought of as so taboo, occult, or witch-like, then she would have eventually come into her trust of her connections to her Linda. She could have learned to use silence and practiced continuing to be with Linda's spiritual presence as she lived the remainder of her life. I envision that she would have been able to find so much more joy within her days had she been guided to this way of knowing. For once our hearts settle down from a trauma of loss, we can once again come to vibrate high enough in order to find our love present and remaining forever.

Indeed, Linda's account of the light could have been welcomed as more of a gift of new knowing within my mother's family had it been received and accepted as such. Their grief and anger towards God shielded them from seeing any signs that she sent to them after her passing. I know that they all believed that Linda was in the hands of the Lord, but they never knew to believe that she was still present in her essence and, in many ways, showing up the whole time.

The divine was alive then, just as it exists now; however, it wasn't openly discussed as anything spiritual, and thus, my lovely Nana held the heartache of that loss for her entire earthly life.

My Nana passed before I came to know my full spirit and the reasons for my journey on this plane of existence. I would have loved to talk to her about my findings, to share with her my feelings and thoughts about all that is soul and the existence of consciousness beyond death while she still lived. I would have *loved* to have been the one to lead her toward the knowings of her own spirit, a light for her to use to heal her sorrows. I have full faith that her energy resides amongst those who she treasured and loved here in her earthly life, me being one of many. I hope that she was welcomed by Linda first and that the light was just as bright for her when her own earthly time expired. She knows her part in my journey, as I know her part in mine. We all intertwine and have purpose in the story of all of our lives.

Being told the story of Linda's life and death in my childhood was the first time I had thought about questioning whether we had a soul that possibly continued living rather than just believing we all eventually died and resided in a heaven or a hell or ceased to exist at all. My personal beliefs were that our energy came to existence, lived as human, and left once again as energy. I always felt deep within that, when we died, we became a part of everything, that we couldn't simply be gone in the end because where then did we come from if we somehow manifested from nothing and returned once again to a void? I felt as though religion and all of its teachings, regardless of which religion we chose to follow, were all meant to guide us toward discovering the miracles that are abundant in life, and attempted to steer us toward loving others and ourselves.

Many years later, after my Nana's death, my mom had experiences of synchronicity where teacups would rattle in her china cabinet on special calendar days. These occurrences happened for years and years, even up until her own death. Mom's doorbell would sometimes chime when no one was there, and upon thinking for a moment, she would be able to equate the day to something and someone significant in her past. I have been witness to some of those occurrences mentioned above and cannot discount them as anything less than fact. She even had an experience once that she could only explain as seeing actual angels with her own eyes, and I believe that she did! She did not know exactly how to reference what she had seen, as there were not words to satisfactorily portray its beauty, but she spoke of it with certainty and without fear of what any other person might think. Perhaps someone else with a less than open mind about what type of being encompasses the skin that we wear outwardly might not have had the opportunity to see the miracle that my mother had that day. One must be willing to believe in the possibility of such occurrences after all, and not everyone has that capacity.

Our soul is *inside* of body. We are Spirit in a suit. We shed our skin upon death, but we cannot ever shed our essence.

Throughout my growing up, my mother spoke of angels, and I always considered them to be real. Nothing about it felt untrue or uncertain in my heart. It just seemed to make sense in my mind that we had to have come from something celestial, something divine, something I could neither see nor hear but could instead feel. I remember her recalling an angel of light hovering over my bed at night as a child. She spoke of the safe feeling and peace it gave her to witness such an awe-striking glow float above me. An angel I believe it surely was. Energy in light. As a child, I called the Source of Life only "God," although I was never baptized into any particular religion, as my parents thought it should be my choice to make once I was able to understand what each one suggested. Now, as an adult, I feel that the name that the Source of Life is given by someone is much less important than the intention behind its following and this magic-like energy. I have referenced this divine presence as many things: Spirit, Source, Consciousness, the Universe, Creation, as well as God, and all of those words do very well at describing Life Source Love.

Love is the purpose of our life after all. Human existence is earthside living, meant for us to experience everything for our own soul growth, and it all boils down to love.

I found my path organically. The steps I took began very young when I believed that I was a creation of the divine. Some of this thought was planted by my brilliant and beautiful-hearted mother, but I like to think that I was born with my knowing not so deeply buried inside, closer to the surface than I realized, until one life-shattering event broke me open to it once again. And now, I am here to bring you closer to your own knowing. To encourage you to sit with your spirit and develop your own relationship with the genuine essence of your own soul.

It's an incredibly journey toward self-discovery. Enjoy.

When All You Need is Your Mom

When all you need is your mom
That reliable care and love
the feeling of comfort and home that is amplified
when you're feeling unwell
The patient and tender touch that brings you cold cloths and sits
silently watching you rest, making sure that it all will be ok
When you need her and her mothering ways
and she is seemingly not there to find
That feeling of emptiness takes a whole other shape in your heart
as a "missing" that does not have any describing verbiage
in this mortal world
Gone but still near
It is Truth, but it is <u>not</u> the same
Sometimes that is harder to remember
Sometimes it seems harder to find
Especially when all you need is your mom

Allie V. Baker

HER DEATH AND OUR RELATIONSHIP

Her death brought me life. The event that seemed to catapult me into a new reality changed the very fibers of how I now exist. What initially was felt so traumatically within her loss has now been replaced with a seemingly whole new feeling in my heart, or maybe now it just beats differently. The years spent wading through my grief have brought about a new feeling to my life. An awakened attention to the simplicity of what life can be. The moments of pause and reflection, the kind of peace and magic that you begin to experience while lending time for just that. A quieting of the soul. A slowing of the moments being lived. And an appreciation for how life could end in an instant.

I loved my mother fully. Yes, we argued and disagreed many a time—as any child and parent does—but in my mind, I loved her more than anyone could have ever loved their own mother. That's how deep my love for her felt to me. It always did. I am blessed, and I am grateful for the kind of mother that she was, and I know not all people get to experience that type of love with a parent. I am thankful that she was mine to have.

Unexpected death. It has turned into the biggest gift of my life. It was the thing that tore me wide open and threw me into the darkness, but it simultaneously helped me rise into the light! I would likely not have opened to spirit in the ways that I feel a sense of home about now. I likely wouldn't have slowed enough to sense the vibrations that energy presents or paused a moment to feel how notes of music can change the feelings that I have inside. I'd surely not be paying as close attention to my intuition as I do when choices and decisions are to be pondered. So much of my life, I would have been missing the miraculousness that is the connection between us and everything that lives had I not lost her when I did, in the way that I did, in order to learn what I've learned and to know what I am to share.

Prior to her death, I was wrapped up in time management and schedule, oftentimes in worry and fear, questioning who I was and what I was to become while here on earth. Unsure of my full purpose, confused of what my contributions were to be, unsure of my true calling. I wouldn't know hope the same as I do now. I wouldn't feel the same joy amongst sadness. I wouldn't have known myself as the soul that I am at my core. I had to learn to trust in the divine timing of all of the pieces of life experience that I was living. I had to choose to trust in that timing, even before any of it made sense to me in any way at all. Before I could heal from this loss, I had to slow myself and listen, record what I witnessed, and restate those findings again and again, and I needed to do so for myself. I had to trust in myself enough to be still and simply pay attention to what emerged genuinely for me. I was telling myself more than I thought could be possible from the perspective of my truth. I just had to learn how to pay attention and listen to the me that was inside.

Recalling My Oneness
– Even on Hard Days

Affirm:
I welcome today's feelings, even though they are heavy
I hold space for my own acknowledgment of my heartbreak
I choose to feel my emotions, and through feeling them,
I release any hold that my sadness seems to have over me
I allow the expulsion of these lower energies to take place through tears,
words on paper, with physical movement, and with prayer
I recall the promise of Joy that is bountiful and awaiting me
within my heart space
I take ahold of that vision and revisit the peace-filled soul that I am
My divine existence remembered, my oneness recalled
My heart calms, my breath kept slow,
and there again, I find you've never left me
Not for One second

ANGELS AND PRAYER

We all have a divine team of support. They are our angels, and they are assigned to us before we come to inhabit this human existence in flesh. These beings of love are available to support us at all times and through any experience or circumstance within our life. They await our request for aid and are always willing to share their knowledge with us. These carriers of light and the purest of loves are available for us throughout our entire earthbound days. They are available for us to become close with and are always able to be counted on.

They are consistent and unwavering, always. They do not discriminate nor do they judge.

Praying to our Creator and to our angels can be a very powerful practice. In this context, I use the word "prayer" to describe the flow of communication from you to your divine team and Creator. You do not have to call it prayer if you choose not to. It does not matter what we title it—or how it is done, for that matter. You could speak it, think it, sing it, write it, using any verbiage that is yours. Your thoughts and feelings are the code of which all your prayers are transcribed for the divine. All that prayer has to be is authentic and genuine, coming from the deepest parts of your soul and spoken from your heart.

Call out to your angels any time you feel that you need support. They hear you always; they listen well. There are literally angels well equipped to teach you on any topic and to help to guide you towards the best choices for your soul's evolution. They are there to help heal you, and to help inspire you. There are angels that exist for quite literally everything in life. Motivation, forgiveness, health, addiction, patience, finances, strength, growth, protection, love, anger, fear, acceptance, joy, grief; the list is endless.

Recognize these divine forces and allow them to have a place in your life. Use prayer practice often as your direct call line to them. Be open to the divine's potential and be sure to share vulnerably with your angels, as they already know your challenges. Then, be open and listen for the responses that they send. This response will likely be more akin to a feeling than that of words. It will be a swaying of thought or a knowingness of sensation. A response may appear as an immediate warmth or tingling, although you may alternatively have an internal message plop into your mind or you may dream something responsive in the nights that follow. Trust that whatever you receive, whether symbolically, physically, or otherwise, will be downloaded from the divine to you in the most effective way in order for you to notice. Remember the necessity of first believing before you will be able to "see," so be sure to believe in the potentiality of receiving your response right from the start.

If you so choose to, you can ask to know the name of your angel or even request that you see what they appear as in your mind's eye. Practicing meditation can assist you in these ways if you choose to dive deeper into those dynamics of your divine team and their light. However, none of those specifics are at all important, unless you deem them to be. Having or not having those details will not make your prayers any more or less impactful. It is simply a matter of personal choice as far as that area of spiritual development is concerned.

Look up, my friends. Keep your eyes toward the skies and pray in your own way. The heavens aren't far away at all. These beings of light will never falter, and they will remain close by you through every storm and celebration you will have in your life. They are your most trusted friends who are along to help illuminate your way and remind you of the home you will one day return to. To divinity itself.

Prayer for Today

*Divine Creator, I ask of you your aid
Allow me courage to listen with my heart's vibrations
instead of solely with my ears
Help me to hear the answers to the questions that I seek
with an open mind and a spirit full of belief
When I falter, remind me to trust in the connection that
I already have to the Universe
Always guide me toward the path that is uniquely mine . . .
for I wish to follow that direction with my whole being
in order to fulfill my destiny
I am grateful and excited to be discovering my higher self
I am witness to all that I experience, and I believe
in my divine light within
Thankful am I*

Allie V. Baker

USING PRAYER DAILY
~ WHEN UPON ANGELS I CALL

There is not one thing in your life that you cannot pray to have support with. There is no "asking for" that is too minuscule to be presented to the heavens. The divine support within all the activities of your life can be easily observed by checking in with your divine team. Try asking your angels to meet you with assistance for whatever it is that you could use a hand with. Perhaps you are hoping to extend love and light toward another human being by the means of asking for help for them. In that circumstance, of course, to their angels you can most certainly pray, asking for their need to be met.

I have put this "call upon angels" theory to the test most recently in my life, and I encourage you to do the very same. Have a sense of wonderment and playfulness about it all, and when confirmation arrives to you in whatever form that it does, be sure to give thanks to the beings of light that assisted with your prayers. This experiment blows my mind every time I test its abundant magic. I use the word "magic" because it truly feels as though it is magical when its arrival to your present moment occurs.

The use of prayer keeps you open to that vibrational exchange between you and your divine team and to your passed loved ones alike, and thus, it becomes quicker to access them and less effort filled to do so with frequent use and with practice. With prayer, you cannot speak in the wrong words. There is no wrong way to do it when you speak directly from the heart.

I recall my daughter suffering from one of her many chronic ear infections for more than a year. We struggled with medicine every time she had any health trouble, so much so that not once did we finish an entire prescription to completion. Every time that she was back in the stages of infection, we would spend more than an hour together twice each day attempting to medicate and resolve this problem for her. It didn't matter that she wanted to get better; her little body would heave every time she'd attempt to swallow any medicine. We tried everything each time to no avail.

One random day, I decided that this could not be the only way that she had to experience attempting to heal. So, with that self-assured determination, upon cutting up her next dose of medication that had never yet been successfully swallowed, I left her and went to the next room and stood silently with my eyes closed. I stood and inwardly prayed to her angels. I asked for them to arrive and gently aid her in completing this very necessary task.

I stated something along the lines of: "Source of love and light, please send my daughter her angels of strength and bravery. Please aid her in swallowing this medication that is so necessary for the healing of her eardrum. Please help her feel calm, protected, and free of fear. Allow her throat to feel open and free of constriction so that she may swallow without worry of choking. Thank you; I am grateful, and so it is."

After finishing the prayer in my head, do you know what I could hear from around the kitchen wall? I heard her counting as she swallowed one piece of medicine at a time. Without tears, free from worry, and with no presence of fear at all. BLESS! Amazed and thankful, I vowed to do the same thing when it was time to give her her next dose, and I did. I was not surprised at all when, once again, she swallowed them that evening without issue! I believe that prayer was the catalyst of that change for her.

I teach my children the power of prayer, the strength of the relationships that they have to the divine and to those who dwell within it all. Everyone has angels. They are waiting to be called upon by you so that they can assist you in your journey. Prayer is a tool in your belt to utilize any time that you need aid.

My daughter is proof that prayer for others can boost our energetic power even higher than we could independently. I implore you to allow your divine team into your life. You must believe in its power before you can see it appear. Be willing to trust that you will be shown that your angels have your back. Use them to help you through life. Ask for support without being afraid of seeming weak. Know that it is not a greedy action to pray for yourself multiple times throughout your day, each and every day and with every action you take, if you so choose.

There are angels for everything, and these knowledgeable beings wish to share their smarts with you. I have prayed to my angels, asking that the traffic be clear for my travels. I have prayed ahead of time for a perfect parking spot close to an entrance of a building in order to make my journey to an appointment easy and stress-free. Upon my arrival, I find exactly what I need without searching for it. I have asked for relief from a migraine and, in doing so, have fallen asleep seemingly instantly, receiving the rest that I needed to feel well again. I guarantee that rest was provided to me quicker than if I had not prayed for aid; I am sure of this. You may not be convinced yet, but wait until you witness answered prayers for yourself.

Hello From Heaven

"Hi, Mama"

"Hello, Baby!"

"Mama, how is it there . . . ? Are the skies Bright Blue and is all WITHOUT Fear?"

"My Dear, I cannot express to you the views that I behold. Mountaintops high and lush grasses below. The views are so much more grand than any you'd know"

"Mama, do you miss me . . . ? As Fiercely as I miss you?"

"Baby girl, I miss you Wholeheartedly, especially your touch. Most of all your Hug . . . but I am still here <u>With</u> you, not watching somewhere from above. Furthermore, I remind you that many things <u>more</u> than Touch <u>stay</u>, and I am so happy to say that I have not gone away. This exit of mine was one ended in flesh, but eternity as Energy is pure in Soul and feels Blessed."

"Mama, how can I Know that you're right by my side?"

"My Love, when you speak to me and feel a Calming Inside. I am Never far and you need only Call. You are the person that I am with Most of all."

THE REMEMBERING OF YOUR SELF

Are you abundantly you? Are you in ample quantity of your truest self, and are you living without fear of who that person is? Maybe you do not genuinely know who that "you" is. Have you taken time to ponder your truths within your life? Are you authentic to yourself and your innermost feelings to the fullest degree possible without having the need for validation from outside parties? Authenticity could perhaps be the hardest part of being a human entity!

Who the you is that you are exactly and how you came to know these things about your "self" is an interesting introspection. How much thought have you put into recognizing the being that you are within your physical shell? The entity that is more than your flesh and outside of the housing for your bones and muscles. Through contemplation of the various challenging chapters that you've lived through in your lifetime, it is in the moments that impacted you profoundly and the situations that hurdled you toward massive growth that are the path to remembering your true and whole self. These experiences lead you towards reconnecting with your own soul. It becomes the revisiting and remembering of the you that is formless, limitless, and timeless . . . the you that is self. Your spirit, your essence.

Our greatest gift to our own being is coming into this place of knowingness and being able to once again recognize that we all have an innate ability to witness being connected to all things that exist because we are connected to everything that exists; everyone is! Your soul is a piece of the Source. A piece of Creation itself. We each possess an internal place of peace that we can visit by only closing our eyes.

Although, I stress that finding this place within oneself only comes to be with a consistent practice of pause and with your choosing to be connected and aware, as we all have this ability within but not all choose to desire coming to its knowing.

Through consistent use of silence and prayer, along with the extension of one's genuine belief in even the things that one cannot see, one will eventually come to a place of awareness that leaves no question as far as the idea of consciousness beyond the body is concerned. However, it is imperative that one mustn't falter in practicing that pause when they come to moments in which they may feel that they've failed to find anything at all. For there will surely be times that one will feel they've gone backwards in their grief healing, become stagnant or skeptical once again, stepped back into an old pattern, or feel lost in the midst of their attempts to uncover their higher self or divine love in any capacity. At those moments of resisting, one must allow the release of the control that the ego is screaming that one needs. We must give over whatever hesitation or expectation we may be having to our exercise.

Provide yourself love and grace to feel whatever comes to the forefront of your heart before once again embarking on your journey of trust toward the divine. Consistency will get you closer to Source. It will eventually become recognizable. Do not give in because you feel you don't have the time to wait to see what is before you. It is well worth the trust and the time, I assure you.

Ask often to see, to remain open and receptive, and request to be the conduit of light for the world. A practice of thanks should also be given for all that you receive as your knowingness unfolds to you. Self-care routines that clear energy fields and aid in restoring the higher vibrational fields that you wish to operate on are imperative. Attention and care must be paid to the body when one feels tired or unwell in order to restore the field and heal and cleanse the mind. This gift to yourself will be the most love you've ever encountered. It will be well worth the price of time as you learn, uncover, and experience your truest self.

Some components of life that we can utilize to help uncover our self and come back to our knowingness are—but are not limited to—the following:

- **Rainfall/Water**—useful for purging, cleansing, and purifying.

- **Sound/Music/Tones**—useful for dissecting emotion, purging, and clearing. Certain notes, tones, or melodies speak to us for a reason.

- **Color**—useful as reference for emotion.

- **Scent**—useful as an identifier of a person or place as well as an enticer of memory.

- **The Sky**—useful to replenish, purify, reignite. A place to cast prayer.

- **Affirmation**—useful as a reminder of who we are in essence and what we believe in. Speaking truths becomes our truth.

- **Prayer (Speaking to Your Angels and the Divine)**—useful as a return to your knowing of faith, reigniting the knowingness that you are loved and cared for entirely. A way to ask for help, for yourself or someone else.

- **Silence/Meditation**—useful practice to learn to quiet the mind, allowing you to hear what is spoken internally from your higher self, or spirit. A loving place of retreat.

- **Traditions**—useful in continuing to foster bonds with those that we love, whether earthside or in spirit.

- **Visualization/Memory Recall**—useful to aid in seeing what is desired to be experienced. A practice that can manifest amazing synchronistic experiences.

- **Gratitude**—useful to keep the signs of the divine coming your way.

- **Purging Emotion/Feeling Grief**—useful to transmute negative energy out of the physical body, allowing space for light love to fill in within oneself. Necessary for healing.

Lead Me

*Spirit, lead me to those who need my light today
Even in small ways, help me to make a difference
Open my heart to the vastness of your love and blessings
so that I may see where I could give more of myself
for the betterment of others
I am grateful for my life here on earth
Help me be a beacon of your love
Amen*

THE JOURNEY HOME

So much of life is learning, experiencing situations in order to learn who we are, what we desire to become, the impact we choose to leave, and how to face the pain of loss. We survive heartbreak and sorrow. We learn how to be resilient and persevere through challenge. We must find and choose forgiveness. Search for love and what joy feels like. Give grace and have compassion. Learn in which ways to trust and in which ways to protect ourselves. We come to know what generosity is. We must find strength, physical strength and the emotional kind too. We must seek hope and allow for our wonderment.

In life, we get worn down, beat down, rejected, and shown the worst of people's intentions. We face questioning, witness anger and violence, deal with sickness and disparity. We experience birth, death, failure, disappointment, even disaster. We learn how to heal, when to hold on, and when to let go. We feel the highs of happiness and the lows of struggle. We learn to teach and how to share. We learn what it's like to support one another and how to effectively support ourselves. We learn the importance of communication, of listening, and even of silence. We have physical, mental, emotional, and spiritual experiences that are all unique to our own life, and we share parts of our lives with many others who are doing exactly the same, only in their own ways.

It is all meant for us as humans to grow. In every moment and with every thought and decision, we live this human life, evolving and changing from one version of ourselves to another and on and on again. Then, upon bodily death, we get to return home with all of the knowledge and life experiences that are of this earth. This human life is merely a lesson on our journey home. Our soul is our essence. It remains alive always.

Remind Yourself Daily . . .

I am a divine being of light.
An eternal soul within this body.
I am grateful to be arriving in my knowingness.
I welcome all signs of my oneness with the Universe.
I send thanks to my angels and my guides for their aid.
I remain open to synchronicity and the path of miracles.
And so it is.

A Memory

Today a memory brought me happiness; at the very same time, I felt sad.

I am certainly most grateful for having at least the time that we had.

I am unsure if I'll ever get used to not having you to hold.

But what remains so true to me is that I must be Bold.

Bold enough to share the Truth that love remains through death.

Bold enough to tell grieving souls that they too can survive this test.

The test is of Strength, Resilience, and of Spiritual Growth.

Your lost and most cherished loved one, my dear, is simply not a ghost.

So Breathe slowly through your sadness, release your tears, and allow your heart to Calm.

Feel it for yourself, my dear; they are with you always.

Most certainly Not Gone.

GREAT LOSS AND THE CONNECTION THAT REMAINS

Love and Death

It only makes sense that, if we have been fortunate enough to experience great love in our lifetime, then we are absolutely going to experience—and suffer from—great and painful loss as well. Quite often a loss of great magnitude within one's life will lead a person to search for answers to questions regarding life and death if we haven't pondered it already. Are we a living human, or are we firstly a soul born into flesh? Is there really an afterlife? Heaven and Hell? Or, when we die, are we just gone, extinguished entirely? When death comes for someone we know and love, some people may look closer for God, some choose to learn about the assortment of religious followings found around the world, searching to find one that fits with what feels right deep within themselves. Those people seek to find answers to life and death that stem from a religious standpoint. Others may direct their search more toward science, choosing to comb through various studied and documented findings on consciousness and death. Others still may lean into their search through more spiritual insights, sourcing reputable mediums, speaking to people who have had their own NDEs or spiritual experiences, and reading books by clairvoyants and other spiritual practitioners alike. The grieving person often longs to reconnect in some way with their beloved person or at least to find out if there really is a place that their loved one has gone to outside of this physical life. It matters to them now more than ever, with their loved one having transitioned from this life.

Various books containing studies of scientific findings dating from many years ago and right up to this present day will provide a questioning human many an answer to ponder when it comes to the afterlife and what happens to our consciousness after we die.

If you are at all intrigued, do your own search on near-death experiences and observe the amount of recorded cases there have been throughout history and notice their commonalities. I found some of these published papers and books on NDEs to be some of the most interesting reading of my life. Books, for example, by the philosopher and psychiatrist Raymond Moody who had his own near-death experience, or neurosurgeon Eben Alexander, who did as well, are wonderful and informative books if I were to suggest a few.

Most of us seem to search for answers to some of our most profound questions during our biggest heartbreaks. The year that I lost my mother, I buried my nose in enough books to feed my longing for her and my questions of the world that I knew was there but could not see. Yes, I had believed my whole life that, in death, we would return to "being Of and Within it all," but once it was she who had died, I felt that I had to have better proof of these self-known answers. I learned a great deal as I read. I practiced working through my trauma and releasing the hold that my grief had on me. I needed to do so in order to heal. I felt the disparity, dug in, and purged, and I did so again and again. I cried oceans of tears as I leaned into the pain of my heartbreak, a practice I still continue to work through whenever my grief revisits me, and arrive again it will! Working through grief is tender, painful, and exhausting, but your grief will be present either way, so learning to heal through it is ever so worth it.

Now, realistically speaking, there is likely no point at which grief will not ever arrive again for me. And any time it does, it will likely impact my spirit to some degree. Even after all the effort I've put in to healing, it will appear in flits of a moment and within a memory from time to time as I live forward. That is OK by me, as I deem it the currency of my love for her. It reminds me in that moment to pause and seek her in spirit. To take a moment and connect my heart space with hers so that I can feel the connection of our love together again. The integration of grief in one's life does not change the occurrence of that loss, after all; that is why sadness and longing can arise for us at any point in our future. I loved her exceptionally, more than any other, and therefore, I will forever miss her physical person, obviously. I do not, however, have to be without her essence.

I believe our experiences of loss are meant to make us appreciate life and love. We grow stronger and can become more solidified in the knowingness of our own soul as we walk through these losses if we so choose. These massive life transitions can wake us up to the vastness of our own individual existence as well as to the limitless bonds further than earth that we share with the divine eternally.

It seems that the more we can lean into the pain of losing someone in flesh by choosing to feel the emotions of loss when they arrive and then by working to release those emotions instead of holding tight or suppressing them, the better we can begin to heal and can more easily come into the finding of our own soul self. We absolutely live alongside of those we love in spirit. If we choose to look, we will feel their energy for ourselves. Souls who have existed in human form and have since passed are as near to us as requested, as are our angels, our divine guides, and Source as well.

While seeking the more spiritual answers to our pondered thoughts and as our hearts heal from grief with the passing of time and with the consistent use of energy practices, our ability to expand our vibrations and foster continued connectedness reappears to us. Only now, with a calm and peaceful heart, it isn't hidden in fear and sorrow as it was before. Death has made us curious enough to consider the purpose and pathways of possible thoughts and feelings within grief and our healing. We can revisit connectedness as we knew it before our energy was entangled into a mass. It will emerge as soul. Spirit. Light.

It exists, and it's available for you to witness for yourself.

Now, if you are anything like me and you've lost a person that you dread living your life without, you'd likely much prefer the idea of continuing to live alongside your beloved person instead of fully without them. That way, our continuing to live can be rejoiced over as we learn to know our beloved beyond their bodily death. The "living" with her looks different than it did years ago for me, just as your life looks different now "without" your beloved, but I assure you that the connectedness anyone can unearth is just as impactful, meaningful, and purposeful to life now as it was back when they lived. I personally choose to seek out the life-force energy that is in everything that exists. My mother remains close to me, as the essence of the person that you treasure remains close to you. I can feel her arrive to me, and I recognize her easily. You are also capable of learning how to access that connectedness. Grieving people do need some initial time to heal their early grief a little bit before they begin their quest in order to allow their heart to accept the pain that they feel and in order to learn to let that all go. Be gentle and gracious with yourself during your early grieving days, you are fragile and in need of your own self-love. By the way, early grief can be defined in a timeline of years instead of weeks or months, so don't fool yourself into believing that your healing is taking too long or that you should be further along than you are.

Grieving the finality of my mother's physical life and absence of body while simultaneously choosing to acknowledge the continuation of her soul led me down a path that deepened my spirituality threefold.

I began practicing pause consistently and using prayer as a means to welcome and witness my own grief. I would name it, feel it, and release it outwardly to be transmuted and sent back to me as light. That is when I noticed the magic-like occurrences start to happen. We all have the potential to access spirit. That connection to the cosmos and all that is available for you to practice at any time, and it is learned from the answers found within your own heart.

Eventually, we will all wake up to the knowing that we are soul. We will all return to existing together and within everything again someday.

Spoken from Your Beloved

For now, you feel you are broken
sometime later you'll heal
Once your healing times come
there shall be a reveal
For when your heart quiets and your tension subsides
you'll be able to realize that my energy's Alive
My death is only of body
I remain very near
to feel it yourself you must release all of your fear
You do not have to lose me, as we are Forever close
My form is of Energy, so you will not see a ghost
If nothing else, darling, Believe and give Spirit your trust
You'll know that it's me! In time, you will see. My soul is Free

DESIRING CONNECTION
~ PRAYER

If I forget to look up, help me to raise my gaze. I feel the opening of my chest as my chin rises.

I feel the sun on my skin. Help me to Breathe.

When my heart is aching in your absence, help me to find peace. Remind me how near you truly are.

Help me to feel emotion and to allow for its release. I do so by pushing energy into the ground through my feet or by allowing tears to flow out of my eyes.

Spirit, gift me the knowingness of your presence today and please do so in undeniable ways. Arrive for me recognizably, show me signs I will resonate with, and help me to see them so that they do not pass me by.

Remind me throughout my day that it is in the stillness that we find ourselves and our answers.

I will pay attention in my heart space for what I will know to be true. I will consciously choose not to question what I uncover within myself, and instead, I will give thanks for the presenting of these signs to me. I know that extending gratitude and belief will bring those signs toward me again and again. Thank You!

I believe in bonded love and its ability to last forever and, as my life now holds a new way of coming to know my beloved again, I am determined to foster and grow in this way together.

I pray that my spiritual reality, where we all exist united as soul energy, shall appear to me nearer than before as I expand myself to feel the love energy exchanged. I, in return, give thanks to my Creator and to my many divine supports for assisting me with learning how to listen within my heart. And so it is. Amen.

GRIEF, HEALING, AND FINDING YOUR SOUL

Becoming open enough to be spiritually receptive in order to find the true callings of your soul will prove to be a growing point within life that, if chosen to be fostered, will have you putting forth a great deal of effort. Just as with any chosen practice, you are not going to wake up one day and happily find that you have extra time afforded to you in which you can easily insert daily spiritual exercises. If you desire to emphasize your connection to the peace and joy that one's own knowingness brings, then you have to choose to make the time to be silent, to meditate, to pray, to be away from electronics, to be out in nature, and to provide yourself time to be alone in simple solitude. A person must have the intent to practice with their spiritual tools and then follow through in a consistent manner, extending patience to oneself when feelings of doubt arise, when feelings of not advancing in experience fast enough come into play, or when they wind up feeling hurried along by themself or others. As humans, we want results swiftly. We desire to find the endpoint and master the skill. We want to do it and do it now. Yesterday, really, if we were to be at all honest. But while on the path to rediscovering your own soul, you must surrender to the be-ing of it all. Meaning surrendering to the flow and unfolding of life as it manifests in the moment that you are experiencing. You see, the release of your need for control and your openness to receive love and light from the divine is required in order for you to arrive at your own knowingness.

When or how is best for you, I do not profess to know, but indeed, we each know for our own selves the answers that we seek to find. We must only choose to patiently inquire about it and then to listen with more than just our ears for the reply from our higher self.

All will likely falter in the start and will perhaps feel that they've learned nothing at all about their spirit and have advanced in no way during their moments of retreat. However, those who continue to seek to practice internal silence consistently through those feelings of blockage and those who remain steadfast through the many seated times of waiting without expectation will become more receptive and increasingly open to learning what is inside of them. They will come to remember what we all are wholly.

I realize it likely seems odd to you, the idea that you're trying to be allowing towards something that you really have no guided direction with. I suggest that you grant yourself the pleasure of finding your magic-like truth for yourself. Trust yourself to relax into your opening. It will aid you in life, love, grief, illness, and success and help you banish your fears. I am telling you with unwavering confidence that you have the knowledge you need already. You also possess the power to uncover this treasure without the aid of any other person anywhere. Even if you assume that something can never come out of nothing and even if you think that you'd be absurd to believe you would just know how to access your higher self without being led on exactly the way to do so. I am here to tell you that, as long as you genuinely believe you are able to do so, you can and will. Trust the Universe and relax into the arrival of your spirit's timing being unknown to you for now. Let go and let "God."

Remember, "before you see, you must believe it is possible."

Caring for your energy field is vastly important to maintaining good mental and spiritual well-being throughout your practices. Come away from immersing yourself with news, social media, video games, and the like. Cutting back on or removing these vibrationally lowering outlets is only going to better your soul and the connection you can ultimately find to your higher self and to other energetic beings that you love. A joy-filled, less stressed, slower-paced life is created in the moment, with peace. Less or no attention is given to the things that we cannot control, alter, or repair, as with most of the things we would see on the news. Other people's posts on social media create a comparison for the most part led by the ego, which translates to judgment of one's self or others and creates a negative vibrational pull against your otherwise shining light.

The company you take is exceptionally important as well. Especially while on your spiritual path. Vibrating high is ultimately the goal for feeling well and being well within. We have the opportunity to learn what vibrational exchange people's energy provides to us individually by using introspection. We can increase our vibrations by being around those who are light and love and who add to our auric area, while we will become greatly impacted by those we encounter who vibrate on lower energy frequencies than ourselves. This amplifies even more so in larger group settings. If you are going into an encounter and are unaware of how someone's energy affects your own, you are less prepared to shield yourself from obtaining a lowered vibration that you could otherwise have avoided.

Yes, protection can be infused and created with the use of spiritual symbols and geometry or by visualizing a barrier or bubble around you, and those tools are amazing to utilize, but it's more effective when you choose to surround yourself with those who add to your auric field in the first place. That way, you limit the amount of people who diminish and dull it. Now, if you have had an encounter with those types of energies, the ones that pull from your spirit and dim your internal light, then you'll have some cleansing to do. There are many resources on spiritual and energetic cleansing rituals and tools at your disposal. Finding which ones work best for you will require you to source them out and try them each for yourself. The fact of the matter is that cleansing and purifying are extremely important to maintaining our best health.

Each of us have different experiences of grief, as each relationship is unique to us and to our person. Like our fingerprints, no two people's connections are the same. Thus, no one's grief or effective methods of healing could fully be the same either. Some components of grief may be experienced, witnessed, and recognized by many, but the way that we feel, the intensity of emotion felt, the timeline to which we integrate our grief, and the path that we walk towards healing and acceptance vary greatly from one person to another. The best way towards healing and hope for each of us is the way that our heart shows us is most helpful. We must listen to our spirit. That, my friends, is the path to repairing your own despair.

Along your journey, you must remember:

No one has the right to tell you how to grieve. No one has the right to tell you when to grieve. No one has the right to tell you how to acknowledge the massive load of sadness that creates great tension within your heart. You must honor your path through this storm of loss with the same tenderness you would provide to your beloved.

Whether your beloved is your child, mother, father, grandparent, sibling, family, friend, colleague, or pet . . . loss is the finality of physical life. It Is something to mourn. It is a loss that will alter your thoughts and make you question far more than you ever have before.

Once your heart heals some from the physical absence of that person, you can reinstate connectedness with your beloved's essence and foster your love to become even deeper than it was earthside. Your beloved's energy, soul, cannot be destroyed since our soul is comprised of a magic-like state of consciousness.

Only it isn't magic; its reality.

Moments of Longing

There are moments that I long for the presence of your physical self.
I long for it in a way that feels like the suffocation of my heart.
In those moments, it seems like no time at all
has passed since I lost you . . .
and, at the very same time, like worlds of time have come and gone.
That is the contradiction of passing time.

BELIEVING WITHOUT SEEING

Do you personally possess a belief that there is more to existence than only what you and I can see . . . ?

Do you hold a belief that there is More to our present reality than our human eyes can witness? A belief in more than what we can hold in our hands, more than the sounds that we hear and the flavors and aromas we can taste and smell? More than physical touch itself and more than what the three-dimensional world suggests to you? Some people need what they consider tangible proof in order to support and believe in any system of thought, which I can understand to some degree. After all, if we hold something in our hand or see it with our eyes, then there is no question as to whether it exists or not. It seems to either exist or it doesn't.

I suggest, however, that people of all kinds give their spirit a chance to prove its existence to them.

Below is a prayer for the extension of your belief . . .

*This morning, I give thanks for the love and protection
of my Source and of my angels.
Today, I set aside all that I question, and I choose to trust
in the true and unwavering divine presence and its
miraculous power within my life.
In the awareness of my doubts, I ask that I be shown proof of the
existence of the divine and of the connectedness that we all possess.
Provide to me signs and symbols that are recognizable to my
individual human form and assist me with accepting these signs and
symbols as the gifts that they are instead of denying their source.*

Send me blessings that leave me without any doubt,
for coincidence is not purely enough to sustain me.
Keep my eyes open to receiving these gifts and let my seeing
them become the knowing in my heart.
I am genuine in my trust of you, the Creator of all,
and in my divine team of angels.
Thank you, and so it is.
Amen.

This prayer—or any other—can be recited as often as you like. It is a challenging venture, consciously working towards allowing your beliefs to not be overcrowded with human thought. Certainly, no practice of extending your belief will aid you without your intention of it being effective. None will appear to work if you have any doubt whatsoever.

Remember that!

THROUGH OUR HARDEST DAYS

Personally, one of the hardest and most challenging things to remember through my hardest days is not to panic and search desperately to find her. For panic and feelings of desperation are not the ways toward a calm and peaceful heart and, ultimately, not the way to finding her essence here with me still.

When my sadness revisits and my longing for her returns, I must welcome and allow that upheaval into my experience in order to release the energy that it bears. Connection feels clouded, heavy, mucky, or absent entirely when sadness is present. It can make a person entirely forget the reality of continued connection and its plausible existence. An important exercise to engage in when that panic state presents itself is to redirect oneself into feeling the emotion and its arrival. It can help to name it or to recognize its source of arrival and then to actively release it. In whatever manner best suits the expulsion, whether that be through tears, actions, words, or otherwise, it is imperative that it be purged.

Only then, after feeling what comes to the forefront of my heart, can I slow my panic-like feelings enough to hold peace in my center and to once again draw on energies that allow me to vibrate higher. Practices of silence, prayer, movement, gratitude, visualization . . . they all assist with my becoming peaceful and open enough to feel her love arrive for me again.

Sitting down in silence and just being with whatever arrives is much different than sitting down and trying to make some connection happen. Exerting too much effort into attempting to create a connection with the essence of our person is a sure way to fail at finding it. Since it may be one of the things that we want the most of all, we should avoid the pressure of that search. Too much effort or too much trying can become a great source of disappointment, fueling our expectations in an unrealistic way.

After having lived through a tremendous loss and while actively missing our person, we can feel almost hurried or in a panic-like state, as we desire so greatly to navigate our connection to that loved one still. Of course we long to have that connection right now, in this very moment. We want to know with conviction that our beloved still exists, and we want to understand and bear witness to their essence immediately, not tomorrow or next year. We wish to know that they are well and that they are with us wholly as spirit, and we'd appreciate confirmation of that straight away, as it feels as though our heart cannot stand to be without them any longer.

We must remember in these moments of pining that it takes patience and practice learning our ways, for ourselves as well. We will need to repeatedly remind ourselves not to overprocess thought or to have any expectations of the ways that our connections will appear. Instead, when you practice pause, be silent within yourself and do not seek out a particular outcome. Your unique ways of understanding how the universe answers you will unfold in good time.

Pray often and be vulnerable with your feelings. Be open to sharing with your divine team all that you carry in mind and heart and, most certainly, be welcoming to finding your peace through your living forward. Be willing to let go of your need to feel in control of how life will unfold and of how you will come to your knowing of self. Believe it is possible so that you will be guided to see truths and miracles every day and in areas of your life you might otherwise overlook.

Do your best to refuse the desire to dissect and define that which you experience but may not be able to explain. Your feelings of knowing will be credible enough to satisfy you once you arrive there. Just be alive and be trusting of your soul's divinity. You will notice that eventually you will find the connection that you were looking for. It will appear when you are fully allowing, when you've given time and space to yourself to figure out your own ways of connection. Your magic will unfold itself to you, and you will know with conviction that it is in their presence that you stand. Your connective bonds with those you love remain always.

PLANT YOURSELF

Step outside and place your feet directly on the ground.

Pause a moment. Breathe deeply and slowly, filling your lungs. Wiggle your toes. Shake out your hands. Move back and forth on the soles of your feet, feeling your balance adjust in order to center yourself comfortably into your midpoint.

Take the time to feel the earth beneath your feet and root yourself into the ground below. Envision your own root system emerging from your soles and spreading out deeply into the earth's soil below you. These roots are strong, keeping you grounded, solid, and immovable.

Welcome the confidence that this visualization brings. Know that you are tethered to this earth life safely, that you are connected to mother earth and are held in her love, even when it may feel like you're losing your grasp because of life's hurdles.

When grief arrives into your now and at any time that you feel unease within your life, through any challenge and within change, you can utilize this practice of planting yourself, so to speak, into the now that is presently upon you and thus leave behind your worry and sadness. This grounding can halt your processing for a moment, much like meditation can, and allow you to just be present, as the earth will transmute your energies. Trust that, with your feet planted firmly and with roots deep within the ground, you are safe to open yourself up to what lies before you in spirit and in soul.

Envision releasing a greyish flow downward into the earth until you see that stream run dry. Then, when you feel the time is right, without rushing through the exercise, envision a light beam opening up from the sky and connecting with the top of your head. When doing so, you will be accepting the light of love and all that is good. This Source light will refill your essence with high vibrations. It consists of nothing more nor less than all that is within love's creation.

Surrender your doubts and trust in the Creator of your life, whatever name you give that force, for surely your angels and guides will light the way towards your knowingness and soul connection with frequent use of this practice. This is a method of spiritual self-care that is necessary for your well-being, especially when on the hunt toward recognizing your own soul and its ability to recall its divine nature.

Trust the words that come to you during prayer; they should feel comfortable and organic. Also, be sure to trust the places that you are drawn to utilize while in these processes. Your soul will guide your journey. Relax into being guided by what is authentic to yourself.

Prayer from the Heart

I trust the universe and its divine timing within my life
I know and recognize that I am an eternal being
who is capable of greatness within myself
I give my worries and troubles to my Almighty and give
great thanks for the peace sent to me in return
I will practice pausing and becoming silent for a moment
each day and will take time to feel the love exchange
between myself and the Universe, my Creator, my angels,
spirit guides, ancestors, and my loved ones
I will not doubt what I see with my heart and beyond my eyes,
for I feel the truth of eternal love within my soul
I emit vast love and welcome the energy of all
that is good into my day
Grateful am I

Allie V. Baker

CONNECT YOUR HEART SPACE WITH YOUR LOVED ONE

In moments when grief overtakes you, be still.

Whether you lost them today, a mere few days ago, many months ago, or even years ago, try this meditation to connect your heart space with theirs.

Sit with your feet flat on the ground and with a tall posture.

Close your eyes and breathe slowly, in and out.

(Choose to breathe in and out of just your nose if that feels most comfortable; the emphasis is on whichever way feels less forced.)

Spend a few long seconds or minutes in that breathing focus only.

If thoughts or emotions surface in your mind while you are breathing focused, try visualizing the word "breathe" in your mind. Hear your internal voice say the word "breathe" and watch the letters slip away from your mind sight and feel your body relax even more, allowing you to once again simply breathe.

Should more thoughts or feelings emerge, repeat the above process until you are feeling peaceful, relaxed, and still. Do not rush this process. Enjoy it.

When you feel ready to proceed, envision a beautiful green hue surrounding your chest and feel its warmth increase around your heart space with each inhale and exhale that you take.

Once that green hue is consistent in vision and feeling, in your mind's eye, picture your loved one. In the most perfect image of them to you.

They are happy and well, and their chest glows with the same vibrant green light as yours.

Their stunning green glow flows then from their chest to your chest, and as it does so, it intertwines together with a marvelous increasing radiance. It travels back and forth, dancing in between the two of you like a heavenly solid string of connectedness.

That is your love! You can see it right before your eyes. You can feel its tangible warmth.

(You have placed a color attachment toward this feeling of love that allows you to view it when you meditate.)

You can watch that flow between you exchange for a few minutes. Relax and enjoy it fully.

When you feel called to do so, speak internally to your loved one and tell them that you love them. Thank them for always being near to you and feel the gratitude emerge from your heart and flow into theirs, all within that green luminosity.

Retract your glow slowly back into your heart space when you feel joy. Turn away from your beloved person in your mind's eye and allow the sensations of the present moment to arrive to you again. Observe the solidness of the space where you sit, hear the noises of your surroundings, and welcome feeling your posture become aware of the reality in your current time/space.

When you feel ready to do so, slowly open your eyes and smile. Know that your beloved is also smiling and feeling the joy of the love that you share together at the very same moment that you too are feeling it.

They are grateful to have connected their heart space with yours once again.

Love is eternal, and it remains unchanged, always. Even when you aren't actively practicing this exercise, when this glimmering glow isn't being subconsciously viewed, it remains present.

You can repeat this meditation anytime, anywhere. It will help you feel the bond that continues between your beloved and yourself. As with anything new that we attempt, initial teachings take practice to get to a place of knowingness with. However, I promise that, if you lean into spirit and bring yourself to practice this meditation when your heart feels like it's torn in two and you're desperately missing your person, you will feel it. You will come to know that your love remains . . . as do they!

Cord of Connectedness

*Are you looking too hard to find me
when, really, I am right here
You strain your eyes and listen hard,
waiting to actually hear*

*You are forgetting it's all subtle,
the signs that you can feel
Warmth, Tingle, and Vibration
All point to what is Real*

*It's like learning a New language together,
committing to patience as we go
Our cord of true connectedness
most certainly will grow*

Affirm . . .

I awaken my spirit to the divine magic within and around me.

I am open to witnessing the signs sent to me to solidify my knowingness of eternal life.

I cast aside my doubt and replace it with genuine trust in my Creator, who is the source of life.

I will speak to my angels and guides as though they are my most trusted friends, for indeed they are.

I am free to release my fears and worries to them, for I know they have the strength and capacity to carry my load without any trouble.

I am a divine soul who is filled with the light of love and all that is good.

This light protects me from darkness, always.

I am capable of witnessing a magic-like connectedness with all of those whom I love.

Whether earthside or in spirit, I recognize that we are all eternally connected. For I am soul.

THE TIMING OF IT ALL

We could all do well trusting a little more in our own divine timing.

Sitting back and saying that you trust in the meaningful trajectory of your life is one thing, but do you actually? Do you fully trust that there is a path and a specific purpose for your life? Do you feel that the timing of events and circumstances are divinely orchestrated and that they are laid out to guide you toward the greatest evolvement of your soul within this earthly experience? Do you believe that you impact people each day of your life, perhaps for reasons that you may not be privy to in the present?

Each day, we are asked to trust in our higher selves and step again into our living forward. As we attempt to believe with conviction that our life is purposeful beyond what we feel is great and meaningful, we hope to learn a great deal from the lessons and the heartbreak that we will each experience in between the joyous and wonderful parts of this life. We hope to make a difference and leave an impact of positivity on others while doing so, and with trust extended, we desire to know that there is a purposeful reason behind our greatest losses. That gives us enough hope to continue.

We seek out the reasons for our unease, for our moments of anguish, our suffering, or for our lost faith. We hope to confirm in our search, that all parts of life are valuable, even within the most unfair circumstances. We seek to know that our spirit is eternal and that even the shortest life lived has given the world a special gift of faith, of love, and of growth before its apparent end. The reality is that each day lived is an experience lived on our journey home to spirit. We are only housed as human for so long.

Trusting in the timing of Creation can make our patience feel stretched and often make us uncomfortable. The end result of our human living is that divine timing will play out no matter how we attempt to control it. There is a divine order to all of it, so allowing our trust to emerge from within and solidify to us that we are always guided, loved, and sheltered is a practice that can help us feel connected and full of wellness throughout our lives. The struggles and the deeply terrifying, world-altering moments we experience on earth can make us question everything, but after we feel the daunting question of why, we can revisit our higher self and remember one thing: that we are all souls and that it is all purposeful to existence for us all. We will one day be shown the roadmap that led us to our final destination. The end of this life is not the finality of our essence, as we continue on forever. While here on earth, we learn through living, loving, and letting go. When existing in spirit, we encompass all of those knowings and even more.

Extend gratitude to the Universe for your life and for the lives of those that you love. Whether your beloved is on this plane of existence or another, the lessons, blessings, losses, and joys are all occurring for you exactly as it is meant to be. All in divine order and all in divine time. There is no controlling what is meant to be your journey, so you are best to give way to resistance and disperse your feelings of needing to be in control. Lean into the flow of your life and trust that the Universe has your back. After all, along with having free will in your life's direction and choices, you are accepted, guided, and loved upon by your divine team always.

Near to Me

Help me to find you. Arrive to me near.
Near enough to feel you. To sense that you are here.
I cannot do this life without you. With it seeming like you're gone.
So walk beside me steadily. Keep my heart hearing your song.
The world that you encompass lies right alongside my own.
Send me signs and symbols to make me feel at home.
You were the place I came to to find shelter from life's storms.
So please, please help me recognize that your soul has been reborn.
I trust that you pray for me in the same ways I pray for you.
I believe that you're alongside me through everything that I do.
I send you my love always and spend time in silent prayer.
I feel graced with love eternal, and I just know that you're right there.

Call Out to Me

If ever you're in despair, call out to me
Tell me of your sadness, although I hate to see you cry
Release all of your fears to me, speak of what you feel inside
For I have never left you
and when you call, I'm there
Open up your Heart
and
Trust your Soul
You will find me Near

INTERNAL SILENCE

Like the Otter laying back and looking towards the heavens, you too can find your Soul in the Sea of Connectedness . . .

Let's pause a moment to reflect.

When you close your eyes, what do you *see*? What do you *feel* when you are not stimulated by visuals in every direction? Would you use words like nothing, darkness, blank space, emptiness . . . ?

Have you ever felt the intensity of the calm that is available and present within you inside the small action of simply closing your eyes? This calm is reachable to you no matter where you are, and it has no reason for the management or time or space. It does, however, take practice to strengthen your ease at finding and possessing it.

Practice pausing for reflection by raising your face to the heavens and aligning with the light of the sun. You can stop your processing briefly to feel yourself breathe. Always smile, just for one second, and as you do, imagine the warmth that you feel from the sun as the web of Creation's energy. A web that connects you to the universe and to all that is and ever was.

If you look, what color is the web of flowing energy that you see? Record what you observe.

Anytime that you feel anxious, unbalanced, worried, overwhelmed, overcrowded, or unsure, pause and close your eyes to witness internal silence. Feel the calm emerge from inside of you, breathe past the struggle and away from the angst, and set the intention to release the held tension freely into the universe with each inhale and exhale. Do so by thinking or saying what you intend to no longer experience.

Just be in this moment. Standing or sitting with your face to the sky and in the light of the sun is best, but nighttime or even cloudy days can do the job just as well. Looking upward at a ceiling also works without needing much practice. The direction of up is just as significant as the light is for this practice.

Whether you're on a bus filled with people, at your desk during work hours, outside doing yard work, in bed alone, or in the company of another person or of no one. Whether feeling happy or sad, angry or tired. Even when being sick, feeling well, having injuries, or healing. Internal calm is there for you to take ahold of, anytime, anywhere.

Peace is within you always, even when you feel great upheaval. Allow that peace to be with you. Close your eyes and practice your pause. Reflect and take yourself within. Inside your closed eyes is a place of refuge that no one can remove you from. It's quite a wonderful practice to use to combat anxious feelings and to quiet our ego mind. It lends comfort to grief and gentleness to sorrow. It's an easy friend sent to relieve you of your aloneness, for you are connected to everything and always have been.

Once again, peace and internal calm are available to us all, and you will uncover the way to them for yourself. They arrive with the help of your own soul and are uncovered as we reflect on our own soul's journey here on earth.

Beloved

I feel a calm warmth wash over me as I sit in silent prayer
I raise my face towards the sun and feel that you're right there
You're standing alongside of me, smiling ever so wide
Embracing me with arms wrapped tight,
as though there was never a goodbye
I close my eyes, I slow my breath, extend my arms toward the sky
It's in moments of this solitude that I know you are nearby
I am grateful for this Knowing
To share with All the world, I Vow
that our loved ones lost to earthly death
Still exist within our Now

Allie V. Baker

HAND OVER HEART

Peaceful state exercise:

What does peace feel like within your heart? Have you ever considered such a notion? When you sit silent with yourself, what feelings arrive at the forefront of your experience? When entering your self in a moment of anxiousness or worry even, can you work to seek and find the calm within your center? Hand over heart, sit still and, with silent, slow breath, feel your heart beating beneath your palm.

Your soul has the magical potential to exist in a peaceful state, no matter the circumstance or emotion in your current reality. In the circumstance of grief, peace may seem like an impossible feat. However, if we are in good practice with pausing, praying, and welcoming peace when feeling anxious, stressed, heartbroken, or lost, when we revisit these practices often, we can better cope with life's adversities.

Placing your hand over your heart is a great way to center yourself into your breath. Use it to bring you out of the three-dimensional world and into the peaceful and capable now within yourself. Trust and surrender your desire to control emotion while in your peaceful state. Notice your disassociation to it. You are not the feeling. It is just that, an emotion. You can choose to recognize and release whatever emotion it is that you feel and once again just sit with silent openness. Have the willingness to witness whatever will be instead of dissecting whatever you think is or isn't. It certainly takes practice to remove your thought processing from your ego mind. Practice doing so with silence, and your calm will appear faster each time that it is exercised.

The only giver of your peace is, of course, you. Gift yourself the practice of release by surrendering, using prayer, and gifting yourself pause with hand over heart. It will bring you closer to Spirit. All of us are connected. If you seek to find your magic held within, you will see the beauty of your life unfold in ways you hadn't considered beautiful before.

Love Eternal

Free me from my yesterdays
Release me of this pain
Remind me I am worthy to not relive that hell again
Help me breathe my breath out Slowly and hand it all to you
Life and Love are Eternal
I am grateful to know this Truth
Still, some days, my heart cries softly
and I feel encompassed with despair
It is then that I reach out to ask again
"please show me you are there"
It takes some time and patience, but with attentive care
I recognize that you arrive for me as though you stand right here

MUSIC AND ITS TONES

Musical tones can have dramatic effects on one's inner spirit. We can use them both to raise our vibration and to allow our stagnant energies to move freely again after being dulled and drug stickily through the ego's thoughts and unrealistic timelines. Music holds power. With its notes, a song can send you on a journey of remembering. It can assist with the release and transmutation of emotion; it can neutralize an anxious mind or amp you up when you're needing a lift. As such, it is always important to select your music carefully. More carefully than you would think, perhaps. Especially when you are in a vulnerable state.

The energetic flow that music produces can tangibly alter your zen and the way you feel. If we break down music as a whole into its smaller, more precise components, we find its tones. Even a single tone itself can impact what you experience, how your frequency vibrates, and even how you respond to stimuli. Give the next experiment a try to see for yourself the response it can call up inside of you. Be willing to take time though. Really avoid rushing. Give pause for the experience of the sound itself before you look for your body's reactions, and as always, record what you observe.

Experiment:

Listen to one note on any instrument. Spend a few generous minutes with that note, the tone meeting with your eardrums on its own. When you hear the sound, what vibration is sent through to your heart space? How does it feel to your spirit?

Remember, this is observed as one single tone at a time. That tone itself can be repeated, but spend many moments in silence before visiting the next tone.

Now, is this particular tone a calming sound to you?

Does it increase your feeling of joy? What feeling erupts for you the strongest? What emotion is present within your heart?

Do any areas of your body tense up or relax as you listen?

Did this tone induce an appearance of color behind your eyelids?

As for the weight of your physical, fleshy suit, does it feel any heavier or lighter as you listen?

Is your being filled with more energy, or conversely, does it maybe feel slowed down?

How about tingles or buzzing; do you feel that anywhere?

Are there any temperature acknowledgments with any of these sounds at all?

After taking time for introspection with this tone, repeat again with a different one. Just be silent with each and see what you uncover.

So very many things can be noted when you explore single tones and how you specifically, your own spirit responds to each of them. You will find that hearing certain tones will rejuvenate you or assist you in changing your mood. Others will seem to make you react overtly, and you will observe resistance to hearing them and actually feel the pull that they attempt at your energy when present. Music therapy, prayer bowls, tongue drums, and other modalities are ways that we can use tones and their power. You can experience the use of your positive charging tones on your own and in your own way to help you raise your vibration, to keep you grounded and mentally well.

After doing this experiment, you are able to better recognize and thus avoid sounds that bring less peace to your spirit, keeping you more in harmony and flow. Once you've completed the above, you can then have a listen to some of your favorite music, and you will recognize that certain tones are present in the music you have chosen and that you often choose. You'll be better aware of what sounds it's best to be around during whatever circumstance you are living through at the present time. You'll be better informed on which type of music will give the desired emotional reaction you need in any moment. What a smart, observant soul you are!

Our favorite songs can breathe life into our spirit. Hearing them can rejuvenate us from a sluggish feeling, lighten our mood, and make us feel awake and giddy. Other songs can even assist us with the release and purge of our emotions, provided we understand how certain songs reach those deep-seated feelings and regurgitate them up and out of our physical bodies. Songs might arrive to you in synchronistic timing in order to provide signs from your lost loved ones. They can deliver messages within their lyrics and place memories alongside their melodies, and they too are wonderful to try with this experiment. Have a listen to some of your favorites and pay closer attention than normal to all of the above questions. Maybe one song makes you think of a particular person, while another sends you reminiscing about someone else and your adventures together. Dive a little deeper into what it is about these songs that speak to your being. There are a great many reasons why we are drawn to certain tunes.

We can use music together with feeling to heal, release, manifest, celebrate, and commemorate all parts of human life. We can use it to infuse our souls with love and bring about the light when darkness, grief, or life challenges seem to find us again. We can exist in high vibration and revisit the sounds that we ourselves need when we feel our batteries lower. Music can assist us with feeling reborn and purified, ready to continue forward as a soul comprised of divine energy, knowing that energy can be recharged by utilizing a great many things.

The Creator of this universe left us many tools for the advancement of our self: music, meditation, the Sun, the Moon, the rain, movement, prayer . . . all of them are free for us to utilize in order to maintain our spiritual wellness and even increase our divine connection to it and the oneness that is us all. We just need to utilize them.

MY INTERNAL SACRED SPACE
~ SILENCE/MEDITATION/
VISUALIZATION

Sometimes it feels as though I can feel my life flowing within the breeze. As it gently moves over my face, it reminds me that I am alive. That I am here to experience living, to learn from trying, from succeeding and equally from making mistakes. While alive I am to accept change, as hard as that can be, and to grow along with the challenges, losses, and victories that are woven by the choices that I get to make while here on earth. My soul wants me to know that I needn't carry the weight or worry of the world and all of its trials, for that is not for my heart to bear, and it is not for your heart to bear either! Instead I do my very best to only focus on what I can directly affect, what directly affects me, and what IS for my attention, concern, and focus.

When I forget the above and I begin to stress or worry about all of the problems in the world, or the many things out of the nature of my control, I retreat inward. My breath leads me to my internal sacred space, which always feels calm and safe. I remember that I need only breathe in order to get to that space in any moment of my living. I need only to trust that the silence that arrives with each breath can bring me truths about myself that I never realized I knew. I need only to return to myself. To my most whole energy, that which is deepest inside of me.

Sometimes, I simply need a reminder. Something to once again make me slow down and yield to my breath. Today, it was the wind. Tomorrow, it may be a song or a memory. The next day, it may be a smell. A reminder to halt and take that pause for myself.

The practice of retreating within yourself often—even in this very moment and once again soon after—is pivotal in the "upkeep" of one's internal space. Keeping with this practice consistently ensures that you have an easily accessible internal shelter for any time you need escape from a feeling or a situation that you know is leaning toward ego-based, fear-induced living. With enough practice, upon using your breath and closing your eyes, you can arrive at a level of peace almost instantly. These moments of pause and breath do not require hours of your time each day, they only require consistent practice in some small degree.

Attempt halting yourself in order to slow your breath for just two minutes twice each day to start. This can be done while you sit on the bus, before or after a meal, in the tub, or, heck, even while on the toilet! Just make an effort to do it. Working your way up to longer times in silence is a muscle you will grow in time.

Please do not start your journey thinking that any short time spent is at all a waste, as it certainly is not. You'll become more comfortable with silence and meditation/visualization as you go. The practice is the important component, and being consistent in your efforts and usage of this wonderful tool will benefit you threefold.

Your peaceful heart will thank you later when you are able to use this retreat upon feeling any kind of unease. Trust yourself to be guided by the internal cues of your soul.

Near I Stay

I am In and Around all that you see.
Here I am; notice me!
I reside in the wind that blows leaves on the tree.
I arrive in between each note of a symphony.
Firstly, you must believe beyond things that you can see with your eyes, for there you will find the Conscious Energy that can remove our goodbyes.
For death sent me nowhere that is at all far away.
Here I am! Near I stay. Near I stay.

RAIN/WATER

The cleansing, clearing effects of the rain and of any running water are purifying. Standing, sitting, walking in, or being near to the rain can wash any low-lying energetic pathways clean of stuck energies and can revitalize you quickly. Using running water to cleanse and clear while washing your hands or having a shower can promote the same occurrence of filtration to someone's vibration as standing or walking in the rain can. Though the rain that falls from the heavens is full of Light Source Love, which purifies you far more than tap water can because of the addition of energy codes.

A person standing out in the rain receives Source energy that is of magnificent radiance, and although its vibrancy is unseeable beyond drops falling in front of your eyes, its cleansing energy will be noticeable to your spirit. You will not need to see its sparkle nor its glow to witness its brightness with *feeling*. You only need to be present in it or as near to it as you can be in order to benefit from the rain and its happening upon and around you. There isn't necessarily anything more to do than that; things will take care of themselves to some degree. You can certainly add additional details to your cleansing ritual while using the rain to accelerate your purification. Prayer can be incorporated, an affirmation spoken, or an intention set.

It may feel appropriate to recognize and release some stagnant energy through purging, or perhaps you can incorporate a brief meditation or some emotionally representative movement that feels authentic and genuine for yourself. Independent experimentation outside of some loose suggestion creates the ability for the individual to find a cleansing practice that is natural and sacred for themself.

Being anyplace outdoors when it is raining is beneficial to humans as a species. We don't necessarily have to be wet in our clothes, however, in order to cleanse with rainfall. We can be wearing rain gear or using umbrellas. Or if you'd rather not get wet at all, I would suggest finding a covered area where you can still be silent and view the rain while you hear it fall. It is still helpful to your spirit. Sit beside the window in your home without any distracting background noise or stand underneath the porch. The next time it begins raining, if you feel like you could really use some replenishing of your spirit and lightening of your soul . . . go get out in the rain, as close to in it as you can, and try using it to purify yourself!

Witness the difference it can make! See if you feel lighter in your heart or less plagued in your spirit afterward. Surrender your doubts about the rain's cleansing capabilities and trust that you truly are a powerful being capable of harnessing your own energy if you lend trust and patience to the learning of your own soul. You, my friend, have the answers within you, and the tools to care for yourself are available internally and at your fingertips.

Exercises:

- Use the rain when it arrives to assist you with your pause. Listen and really hear its fall. Be silent, not with anticipation of hearing the rain but only to see what it sounds like authentically. The sound of it hitting the ground likely evokes a calm over you. Be with that calm. Sit with that feeling of peace. Observe the rhythmic falling pattern of the rain and envision it clearing out any dim or dark areas of your aura. Replenish yourself as you fill with light from the sky and from within the stillness of your body as the rain washes your spirit clean.

- At a sink, simply rub your hands back and forth together under the stream of water. While you do so, envision its purifying energy flowing over and through your fingers and palms. Keep washing until you feel the stream of water is pure. Say a prayer of thanks for the water's cleansing.

- Near a stream or river? Take off your socks and shoes and stand or walk in that bountiful, cleansing water. Or bend down to run your hands back and forth through it. The main point is to use it!

- The shower is also an excellent place to dispel any grief, angst, or concern. Visualize the water from the shower head in your mind's eye and watch it bring upon you a light of gold or white. Picture that color covering you with its luminescence. It easily pushes the darkness of struggle off of you. It replaces the dingy film of sadness and slow vibration or worry with a layer of light-bearing love that vibrates high and with strength. The drain below filters out that which is not helpful to your spirit.

Rain or the washing of hands or body in the presence of prayer can be very moving. It can be deeply heartfelt and can have a person feeling very close to God/Source. This experience can be profoundly more so when someone is faced with struggle, loss, or massive change in their life. Utilizing the practice of prayer in the rain while asking for a release of emotions can allow us to let go of some recent feelings of sadness and heartbreak. It can allow for release and dispel some of the darkness being held over our heart, at least until grief/loss/struggle revisits again. Fortunately, the next time any of us are hit with an unexpected surprise jab from life's hardest changes, we will have some ammunition to use to aid our broken spirit. We can once again make use of the rain to let go of that which we cannot control and therefore that which we should not be holding on to too tightly. It has been shown that held trauma causes disease, after all, so we want to heal our hurt, not hold onto it for a lifetime.

With practice, any person can begin to notice the connection that being in the rain makes you feel to the oneness that is our existence. It is palpable, if you slow yourself enough to recognize Source energy. You will hear the rain as you feel it and as you see it. Your words or thoughts while praying in the rain and while coupled with intention and mingled with your energy will connect you with the rain itself. It will cause you to vibrate higher within its flow and its fall from heaven to earth and its travels far into the depths of the soil below. That falling rain comes from the same Source that the trees grow from. From the Source that allows the birds to fly, that creates miracles, and that beats the very heart in your chest. The trials of your heart diminish as the waters flow from sky or from sink, and perhaps you cry like the rain falls. Or perhaps the rainwater acts as your tears if you have run out of all tears there are to cry.

Rain/water will always assist you.

Next rainfall . . . get outside!

Say a prayer of thanks for the aid of this rainfall before you set your intention to use it for your cleansing.

"Grateful am I for this cleansing rain. I use it today to rinse from my heart the _____that I feel.

Let me be washed free of my worries and of my fears. Allow me to feel cleansed.

I give loving thanks to this rain for its purity, to the earth, and to my Source.

I extend faith and trust in my Creator, and in return, I remain open to receiving massive blessings from the divine."

In Light and In Darkness

In Light and while in Darkness, dear,
I will find you there.
In Laughter and while feeling Despair,
I will find you there.
In morning time or late at night and to your very heart's Delight,
just relax and close your eyes, and I will find you there.

SILENCE

Silence Exercise:

Stand comfortably. Raise your eyes to the sky, keeping your arms loose at your sides, palms up. Rest your eyes comfortably on a fixed place in the sky. Almost like you're daydreaming.

Allow your eyes to relax and even close if they feel heavy. Breathe in through your nose and out through your nose. Listen to your breath carefully and slow it down with each inhale until you are in a gentle, rhythmic pattern. Notice silence. Notice pause.

Any sounds that your ears pick up, simply label them, release your attention from them, let them fade, and then once again notice silence.

Your breath only and silence.

Let's say a car passes by. You hear it . . . you think "car" . . . release the thought, focus again on breathing, and then you hear your breath only, accompanied by silence.

Maybe you then hear a door closing. . . . "door." . . . release the thought, focus on breath, and then you hear your breath only.

Once you're satisfied with your intended time of practice with silence and you are relaxed within it, take a moment then to look at other things.

Can you feel a breeze on your palms? Notice heat or cold anywhere in your body? Do you have any tingling? How about any other sensations of energy? Can you locate a part of your body that feels something different than the rest of your body?

Any sensation that you witness is because of that silence. That space you provided for halting and being with your self in the now. Your true self is limitless, timeless, and a wondrous being which is connected to all that is. It is emerging for you to better understand it because you've provided it that time. Now, if you provide more moments to pause and be witness to what arrives in silence, then you will become more and more comfortable with the sensations that occur when energy shows up for you. Subtle changes will feel magnified because you're practicing be-ing and not just be-ing, but be-ing you, in your body, without a forced notion or expectation of any kind.

It seems to me that it's the trust factor that holds many people back. How, they think, can I trust something exists when I cannot see it? How can I believe that I have the ability to find my own soul connection when I'm not even sure what that's supposed to feel like? How can I be sure I have enough patience to be silent long enough and with enough consistency to actually make headway with coming to know my self? To the doubter, I would say, perhaps give yourself some grace and then begin to practice casting aside thoughts of needing to see something in order to know that it is there. A great number of things are not visible to us all throughout our days, and yet, we know they remain constant and that they exist.

Radio waves that emit signals and sounds exist around us continuously; we can't see them. Energy has been proven to exist, but it also is not visible. The air we only see when the wind blows, and you cannot look at oxygen. As far as gravity, well, yes, you see the effect of it when an apple falls from a tree, but you do not see the gravity itself. You cannot see thoughts or smells or sensations. We cannot see the universe in totality, and yet, it holds life-forms of all kinds, and its limitations cease to exist, as far as humans can tell.

Truthfully, what you can unfold and become able to witness within the practice of silence can only be unearthed by actually feeling it as it settles through your person. Silence can feel peaceful, especially when we are purposeful in slowing ourselves down enough to render it a gift of pause, and so we begin to feel less pressure toward hurriedly filling the passing of time as we know it. How we are choosing to fill those time gaps in our day becomes more apparent. Silence and the slowing of your thoughts can help you surrender to the parts of you that exist as the quiet energy inside of you. Your soul is your spirit as you are and as you always have been. Though it is a silent and invisible form, it is all-powerful; it coexists and collaboratively creates along with the Maker of the Universe.

Any time given to oneself to simply exist in silence is extremely beneficial. Have those quiet moments be your meditation. Even if you cannot find time to sit still, take two minutes or so and focus on breath. Do it each day. Then, look for other activities you can do quietly, in silence. Do the dishes in silence instead of humming a song or listening to the TV in the background. Drive to and from work in silence. Do your house chores silently. Walk the dog without headphones or workout without noise. Every silent moment adds to your inner calm bank like fresh water to a dried out, thirsty plant. It's truly an experiment you ought to try for yourself. See how thirsty your spirit roots become to have more of the crystal-clear energy that silence provides.

Try changing the amount of each day that you exist in silence. Can you alter some of your daily activities to now happen quietly and yet still be productive and comfortable being present in that silence? Can you notice that, as you increase the amount of silence you exist in, the less anxiety you feel less often, the more peace you can recognize even without the effort of looking for it, and the more calm you can find within any circumstance?

Try these changes for a week or even just a few days and see how your spirit feels lighter:

- Do not watch TV
- Do not view news programs
- Do household chores without any music
- Drive to/from work without the radio on
- Run errands without chatting on the phone
- Exercise without your headphones in

Listen to the lovely things and even the not so wonderful noises that you'll notice when you're silent. I've always found it incredible to recognize what I hadn't been hearing, because of all of the noise I was keeping around me. I feel lighter and more at ease within silence. My chores and tasks feel more like acts of service towards myself and those I love when I complete them silently instead of them feeling like mundane tasks that I am not too happy to be engulfed in. The more I was silent in the times I could instil that for myself, the more I came to know the "who" that was beneath the surface of my human skin. My soul calls out to me to share with you the truths I've found within pause. The truths that you too will uncover if you trust your self to show the way. Aid yourself with the gift of silence. Pause to hear the answers of your heart. Take the time to just be. Then, you will see.

REMEMBERING WHEN WE FEAR THAT WE'VE FORGOTTEN

When you recall a memory and then pair it with the intention of experiencing the same feelings that came upon you during that moment of occurrence, you can anchor in the energy of that experience as if it's happening to you today, in real time. If humanness has weighed you down and you are convincing yourself that you've forgotten what someone's presence feels like to you personally because they're "dead and gone" . . . and if that has you worried that you will not be able to recover those feelings of them again, bring yourself back to a memory of you with that person.

Choose a lovely memory. Allow the vision of the both of you to appear in your mind. Feel the happiness, joy, peace, calmness, love . . . whatever emotion that is emitted to you that was experienced in that space/time. Feel it in the ways that make it come alive in your head. Smile through this practice! You do not need to see them in order to know that their presence is right there beside you in the moment of that memory. Notice a contentment settle in your heart space when they've arrived to experience this memory alongside of you.

When we are overcome with sadness, filled with grief, clinging to the past, and generally vibrating low, we have trouble recalling what someone's presence feels like to us without a physical person to see before our eyes. Our brains take over and spew to us information that the body of whomever has expired, and thus, so has the person, but that is simply not true. Our essence, our spirit/soul has no end to its existence. When we forget that connection because of trauma or grief and we panic at some level that it cannot be rediscovered, we must pause.

Only pause and breathe into your heart space, envision a recalled memory, relax into feeling the emotions and energies that were present in that time/space, and then pay attention to your senses. Oftentimes, you'll notice that, as we compete this exercise, other memories we hadn't thought of will arrive too. It is like a gift of remembrance between their soul and yours!

Remember Them

In days when sorrow leads your path, remember them.
Their presence felt like a calm and safe space to hide away. . . .
Remember how their touch felt the very same way.
Remember the way their hair framed their face . . .
and what it felt like to have their embrace.
Remember their smile that induced others to smile too . . .
then remember, my Dear, All of that remains within You.
Remember places traveled near, far, and in between.
Remember all that Was and Is still to be seen.
Remember their Love for you will last forever.
Remember them bright and that you are still Together.
Remember they will show you that they are still there . . .
if you Remember to trust, practice belief, and use prayer.

I Am Right Here

I am right here
I am So near
I see your Tears
I hear your Fears
You feel that "without me" is how you have to spend your years
But I will Rejoice in showing you different
If you surrender and let Trust be your commitment
The Universe is vast with its magic and light
Our own soul energy allows us to Unite

Allie V. Baker

GRATITUDE IN HARDSHIP

Tough and challenging times show up in our lives far more than once or twice through a lifetime. None of us are spared from hardship of various kinds and to varying degrees. When these occurrences present themselves to us, we can feel like shells of utter hopelessness. Lost, hurt, dissolved, absent from our familiar reality, scared, sad, and angry. Those emotions are absolutely relevant to feel within change and when loss or challenge is upon us. In the moments where we can't begin to imagine what could possibly be worse or how things could get any tougher, in those times that we feel we might not survive or completely dread what's ahead within the unknown, processing the lessons that come to us through the hardships that we encounter is best found within the practice of gratitude.

Finding the things that are blessings and miracles even when you are heartbroken and feeling defeated will change your energy and lead you back to some measure of hope, leaving you more able to live forward and adapt as you have to through whatever adversities you are facing. Oftentimes, a person has a vision of what they expect or plan to create within their life, and oftentimes, they'll find that their life becomes nothing like they'd thought originally. I have come to understand and realize that, if we can change the trajectory of our thought—especially when we are within an emotion of fear or sadness—to instead hold forms of gratitude, then we can change the way that things are viewed within that moment and thus change how we feel about living through it. At least for a little while before we will have to self-regulate again.

In the newness of a particular challenging chapter of life, we may have to redirect ourselves back to gratitude regularly. The mind may slip sneakily back to sadness and worry and have us needing to once again consciously and forcefully look for the gratitude within the hardship. It will not feel easy. It will not be a permanent fix to feeling our problems, but it will restore faith that we have many blessings within those challenging experiences.

Trauma senses can be deeply ingrained into our nervous system. They can automatically and immediately deliver to us undeniable feelings of dread and fear that are all too familiar and unwanted. These senses are heightened and appear automatically to us after having experienced a challenging or undesired event, and they can thrust us back into an emotional state that is less than desired. Maybe you can relate.

Personally speaking, after my mother passed abruptly, when I would encounter a new, challenging issue to face within my life experience, one that was not anticipated and that felt unmanageable, I would instantly feel almost panic-like within my heart space. Those feelings would leave me anxious with worry; they would propel me back into the same feelings I experienced through her loss. In those moments, I forced myself once again to think: "Where is the blessing?" "Where is the good?" Always with a mention of "Thank you" when something positive was recognized.

Boy, that can take effort! This practice is darn well hard. When you are in that state of the unknown, when things are different and life is changing, it can seem impossible. Consider increasing your gratitude practices. There is always something to be grateful for. Always.

> Focus on the blessings within the struggle. Let's look at a health challenge as an example here. Let's say that someone you love has recently been diagnosed with a rare health condition. You can shift your fear or worry into massive gratitude that could be found in:

- the discovering of the issue (being able to prevent further decline or provide the care that will best aid the person that you love)

- receiving a diagnosis of the issue (being aware that not all health problems get concrete answers)

- amazing doctors and nurses for care, guidance, and support (these people are walking angels)

- the search for and finding of medications or treatments to aid in management of a diagnoses

- the Information that discovering this health challenge can and will provide for the lineage of a family (which provides the best health care possible for all of them)

On the days that one feels the struggle in their heart a lot more than others, make the gratitude search even more magnified. Put your focus toward what you might call the "smaller things":

- clear weather for driving in order to make an appointment on time
- light traffic during travel
- no construction hold-ups
- a close parking spot at the hospital
- a gentle nurse for blood draws
- hydrated veins for less pokes
- a short wait on lab work results
- appointments in town rather than having to drive far
- medications that make a difference in how our person feels

All of these things, the big and the small blessings, make living forward through an experience much more tolerable. Even though gratitude may have to be executed one step at a time, it is a practice that essentially helped save me from breaking while I navigated the various storms of my life thus far. Gratitude practices help give perspective. They reinstated my hope for whatever it was that the future was going to unfold to us. We would all benefit greatly from searching for and giving gratitude for the blessings within the mundane, the painful, the challenging, and the wonderful, of course.

Once Again

*When the sun sets, we know it will again tomorrow rise
When the rain falls, we know the ground will once again be dry
When a storm blows in, we know the wind will calm
and clouds will part again soon
When nighttime falls, we know to expect the presence of the moon
And so too, we should know that, when life on earth shall end,
our souls return to the spirit world to be together once again*

TRADITIONS

Our treasured people in spirit continue to rejoice in celebration with us during special occasions. Continuing the traditions that we shared with our person when they were still alive in body helps us to stay close to them beyond their death. Can you recall a shared tradition with your person? Which ones come to mind as you reminisce on time spent with them? Then, in what ways can you implement that meaningful or enjoyable tradition into your living now? Can you create space for enjoying that tradition outside of the normal scope of its occurrence? Meaning, can you find a way to implement it into your life somewhere that isn't just on a certain holiday, date, or only for a particular event?

Being creative with ways to include the traditions that we shared with our beloved is a wonderful way to keep them alive in our memory, strong in their spirit-connectedness, and participating in our life daily. Whether that tradition is baking treats or cooking special dishes, there is no reason that we cannot enjoy the recipe, let's say, outside of the season it was intended to be utilized for celebration within. If your special person was known for sending birthday cards out via snail mail, perhaps then you keep the tradition, alter it a little, and begin sending snail mail cards out just to brighten someone's day for no intended reason at all. You can be assured that your loved one is enjoying the act of you sending the card and will also enjoy when the receiver receives it. You see, your person knows that the reason that you sent the card and partook in that tradition was because of them, and the love that you felt when you were a part of that exchange originally is ever present within the act. You've continued a tradition with them in your now.

Equally effective for remaining close to our person is beginning a new tradition with them in mind. All it takes is spending some time thinking loosely of your person. Notice anything that comes to mind to reference them. What memories flood your mind? What symbols represent this person? What kinds of things did they love to do? What were their hobbies? Favorite foods to eat? What did they like to read? Were they a fanatic for a specific television series? Did they enjoy a certain fragrance of perfume or essential oil? Wear a favorite color often? Maybe they had a favorite flower always in a vase on the table? Or perhaps they retreated to a particular place regularly for a getaway?

Whatever comes up for you can be twisted into a beautiful new tradition that honors them and also has them celebrating alongside of you at any time that you choose to incorporate it into your day. You can make these traditions big or small. You can use them frequently or only as a special ritual. It is all your choice and all what you make of it. These little things can hold the most special parts of our remembrance of them. That is enjoyable for all involved.

My Tradition of Love

I've made it my own; the day that you were born to this earth now serves as a time for me to share my Love for You with a complete stranger. My own ritual of Love.

I purchase Orange Roses. I purchase them with You in mind. I know how you Loved that color.

I drive somewhere local. I park my car and wait to feel pulled energetically to someone random. For whatever reason that is and perhaps for no reason at all, I Trust that the pull I feel is going to make a difference in someone's day. Even if only as a small Lift of light in one's spirit and as a gesture of love extended.

I gift them for You, to a stranger. I trust that guided pull that I feel to whomever is a "meant to be" happenstance directed by the Universe. I hold this sacred tradition because You held my world, and now, I must survive it differently because You were Magnificent and there could never be any comparison in my heart. Mostly, I complete this tradition because You lived. You were Mine, and you were Cherished. And so, I do it to Honor You, to celebrate our Love and to extend it outward for others to feel as well.

And as I do so, I feel the most lovely warmth encircle my heart.

Allie V. Baker

Magical Box

If there was a magical box, I would take it away to all of the places that I wish we had stayed.

I would fill it with all of the memories of New, the ones that I wish I could still be making with you.

It would be stuffed full of all of the "Happy New Years," and any new memory could erase all of my fears.

I would carry that box filled with magic and light proudly through every day and each night.

Collecting our Love, keeping memories inside of all of our newest adventures through time.

Now, today, as I raise my face to the sky, I am reminded that Death is Not a Goodbye.

We share a new way to Connect and share Joy, and it feels even better than a child being gifted a toy.

This Magic-like Box holds my Treasures alone; it can feel almost like a true coming of home.

Together we are, even seeming so far, for all of my life you were my one shining star.

You lifted me up then like you lift me up now, the good Lord above has shown me just how.

I am living my life, and with all that I do, I am Grateful to know I still do it with You.

The Voice

That voice in my head that comes through as you,
for it to be you, seems too good to be true.
The days that arrive painfully and seem absent of you
are so very different from feeling us two.
Together for a lifetime, I must only believe
and then simply be watchful to what arrives for me.
Appearing that my "humanness" gets in the way of my "Know,"
but then spirit reminds me that "in that too, I grow!"
It becomes about trust of what we can't See.
It is all So much bigger than just you and me.
And so, my mind wanders to moments with you,
as though you're right beside me doing the things we'd always do.
Those thoughts feel like experiencing all that love that we shared,
then that memory becomes real, and it shows you're right there.

MEMORY SHARING

When you remember a place,
When you recall a time,
That memory is Also Mine

Spirit has let me know that, what I recall, she too remembers.

We share our memories with loved ones the same way we share love energy between one another in warm embraces. This exchange of energy is the same as the vibrational exchange that occurs for memories to be recalled and shared between two people. With bonds of love, when you remember an event or a journey taken together, a meaningful conversation, a milestone experienced, or any simple moment spent with them, they too are holding space for that very memory simultaneously. It's a direct vibrational line that is an energetic connection between them and you in that moment and within that thought. It can be thought of as a type of phone call connection, only instead of one giver and one receiver, the two energies are experiencing or "thinking" of the same thing at the same time.

Exercise:

Pay attention to the memories that you recall without force.

- **When did that memory arrive for you?** Is it a specific date on the calendar? Is there numeric significance with the year? Or with the time on the clock? Is there an anniversary of a special event approaching? Or one that you didn't realize has just passed?

- **What do these memories stir up within you?**

    Emotions of love?
    Safety?
    Hope?
    Forgiveness?
    Security?
    Happiness?
    Excitement?
    Adventure?
    Gratitude?
    Joy?

- **What are the details of the memory?** Who is the primary interaction with? Where does it take place? What are you doing? What was the occasion?

Asking yourself some of these questions when you have a memory slip into your mind can direct you to decoding a purpose for recalling the memory that was sent to you by your beloved. It is a practice of paying attention and then loosely dissecting what could be the underlying message coming forward.

Oftentimes, if we inquire in our minds on the details of the memories we recall, we will find that their specific arrivals uncover a so-called perfect timing that seem to illuminate the purpose of recalling a certain memory when we did. For whatever reason, the divine allows us to have this thought exactly when we were supposed to in order to share that memory with our beloved. Our most loved person often has a lot to do with this interesting happenstance.

At Christmastime

*Tirelessly, you decorated and shopped
and always wrapped after you bought
In our home, you cooked, and you cleaned
You prepared to be Hostess; your aura always beamed
Your smile was infectious through most every day
You made it all look easy in the most effortless way
Your food, oh the flavors, and the smell was divine
and always washed down with an inch of great wine
These memories of Love all remain in my head
I pray that I'll dream of them while sleeping in bed
I sing the Christmas songs, feel the joy, and hear your laughter
Christmas holds you differently, now and forever after*

Notice Spirt

Visit with the Sunrise
You'll notice Spirit there
Close your eyes, outstretch your arms
Feel the Universe's care
Our loved ones never leave us
Their Soul with us can stay
Trust, Faith, and Genuine Belief is set to light your way
Our energy is vibration
Our prayers connect our Love
The ties that Bind us continue past death
As on earth, so as Above

Phone Call

Today, I made myself a mental note to call you,
to share a tidbit of my day
One small memory had come back to me of before you went away
Then my heart reminded me that with angels now you fly
And although that phone call cannot be made,
you Are directly by my side
That memory gave me happiness at the very same time I felt sad
I am certainly most grateful for having at least the time we had
I am unsure if I'll ever get used to not having you here to hold
but what remains so true to me is that I must be bold
Bold enough to share the truth that Love remains past death
Bold enough to tell the world that we can all survive this test
The test is of Resilience, Strength, and of Spiritual Growth
Your most cherished and lost loved ones, my Dears,
are Not just simply ghosts
So breathe slowly though your sadness, release your tears,
and let your heart be calm
See it for yourself, my Dears; they remain with you
and are most certainly not gone

MOVEMENT

This handbook shares the idea of visiting intimately with your own self across many thresholds in order to learn the unique way that your spirit decodes what your body is communicating to you and how your soul interprets what comes through. I have suggested that the time that you spend in silence, speaking prayer, in meditation, energetically cleansing yourself, and visualizing are all imperative tools to use for learning those lessons for yourself. Intuitive movement is another wonderful category to delve into.

Movement can quite literally move your energies. Your intended physical motion can help stagnant low energies become loosened or dispelled all together. Movement can help you begin to raise your vibration when you feel that you are out of alignment with your most peaceful state. Spending time with yourself in order to find out what type of movement helps you alter your energy best is the only way to uncover what genuinely speaks to assisting you. A person can spend considerable time testing various movement exercises individually. It does not necessarily have to be a category of sport either. While one person might decipher that they feel their energy move most effectively when they go for a jog, for someone else, it is dancing, and for another, it is swimming in the lake.

Alternately, for some of us, this movement is of a more condensed description. One that is much more simplified in order to be effective, such as the shaking out of our arms and legs, simply jumping up and down, drumming our fingers, squatting, or swaying side to side. Stretching and slow movement can be as effective to some people as fast-paced, energetic movements are to others. Begin to move in whatever fashion authentically comes to you and pay attention to what your body tells you it utilizes the best in order to determine the best recipe of motion for you.

Movement Exercise:

The next time you feel a less than desirable way . . . be that angry, sad, tired, stressed, anxious, or fearful, begin by being alone with yourself and start to notice the way that your body begins to authentically create movement.

Begin by naming the emotion that you feel in your body. Close your eyes and allow your body to move independently, without thought. Notice what movement your physical body is using to move this emotion at this time. Extend that movement when you've established it. (Continue it for a few minutes).

As you are moving, can you feel the energy loosen? Can you notice the ways that your energy feels to be changing through the use of that movement? Writing your personal observations down becomes helpful to look back upon. As you add to your notes, you will end up with your own dictionary of self!

If you initially don't feel like you've had any alteration in your vibration, try using a new movement until you do notice some degree of change in your body. Then, when another adverse emotion arrives for you, repeat this exercise and be sure to once again name and always record your discoveries. You will begin learning the subtle ways that your body is constantly speaking to you. You will also be better able to use motion to effectively move through your feelings of strife or struggle, helping you to get back to vibing high far sooner than if you hadn't spent any time at all learning this for yourself.

My Heart

It was as though I lost the housing for my heart
in the instant that you left
Your presence felt like Home to me; your hugs were just the best
You were where I went for comfort, to be welcomed and loved upon
And Every day that I awaken, I just cannot believe you're gone
You reminded me of my importance and the gifts I held within
Always with reminders, too, that No one is free from Sin
It felt as though you sheltered me when you lifted me in prayer
You guided me with a tender heart that was always full of care
You'd always forgive me for my Human-ness
and All of my lessons learned
Never once in my whole life did I feel your love needed to be earned
You were then, and are still now, my safe place deep inside
where I am free to just be me, and I Know that gives you pride
I came to you to feel worthy when someone else had made me doubt
You walked beside as I struggled to figure this life out
And so I practice finding you in the space that your spirit now resides
It's all around me in this world and also deep inside

Morning Time

The beauty that the morning brings . . .
Oh! Glorious things, glorious things!
When I stand to silently sing in the Infinite-ness that is my Be-ing,
I welcome to my heart a connection of love.
Sent straight to me from the heavens above.
Although I must tell you, heaven is not up high,
the energy of Spirit exists right alongside.
Alongside us in our every day.
Available to reach in many a way.
Our connections of Love last past death and beyond time.
Our connection surpasses the questions of how come and why.
The sky, oh my! The glorious sky.
It helps me recall the "I" that I am Inside.

ESTABLISHING SIGNS

After a significant amount of time has been spent in silence with yourself, observing your self and recording how you personally notice energy with color and sensation, and after having recorded what you've noticed comes to the forefront of your thoughts, feelings, visualizations, and other senses during those moments of observation, you will have created something of a unique personal dictionary to utilize. You will have created a template through which to better understand your self and your connection to divinity and spirit.

Signs and symbols can be determined with anyone whom we love while they are still alive. Communication with loved ones about these representations can make the connection process after someone has passed far easier to establish for you both since your signs and symbols will only need to be noticed when they arrive to you. For this reason, I suggest striking up a casual conversation about the things that come to mind regarding your relationship with whomever you love. Please recognize that a sign does not have to be a tangible object necessarily, although recognizable and common objects are often found to be signs by those who interpret meaning behind them. Butterflies, dragonflies, birds, feathers, pennies, dimes, and bobby pins are some of the most common signs received from spirit. A sign, however, may be determined to be a symbol that is recognizable from a place that you traveled together before. You could also relate a favorite animal that is always spoken of by someone as being a symbol, a certain type of pet, or an animal that resembles your loved one in appearance, sound, or movement even. The distinct smell of a particular food being prepared can be a sign or the scent of a certain perfume or cologne, perhaps one that your person has worn for years. Signs can be complete songs, specific lyrics or words, common phrases, initials, or even names. Many people consider numbers or sequences of numbers to be signs, and truly, signs can be anything at all.

Of course, there are situations in our lives when time does not afford us to have such conversations in order to establish these signs together with our beloved. Death may have already occurred, or there may no longer be the capacity for verbal communication between you and your person. Whatever the reason for not being able to establish a potential sign prior to the death of a loved one, you do not have to worry. If this is the case for you, please know that meaningful signs can still be established now. All that is required is one's retreat into silence and for time to be spent discovering what signs are authentically given and which would be deemed by you and them to be most appropriate to represent your relationship with that person. Remember when we went inward and only paid attention to the color that arrived to us behind our eyelids and then we decided what that color felt like to us, if that color represented something to us personally, and if it made us think of something in particular? This is the same idea. Retreat with your self and record what comes to you. Genuinely.

You can choose one single sign for representation of a person or many signs combined. The sign(s) can even have various parts to it that you state are required to be present together in order for you to consider it a viable sign. You would need to state the particular details that the sign would need to have in order for it to be deemed specifically so. In addition, please think back to the part of this handbook that spoke of "believing before you will be able to see." For you *must first* believe that the signs and synchronistic occurrences involving those signs *are possible* before they can be available to be utilized by your beloved as such. You do not have to outwardly speak the details of the sign(s). You do, however, have to establish them with full and complete thought, making the connection from the item/symbol to the person themself and to you.

Once you have taken time to establish your sign(s), it is not about searching for the arrival of that sign. It is all about being aware throughout your day in order to notice the sign when it does arrive. And indeed, you will see the signs appear for you. Perhaps not immediately, maybe not that same day, and likely not in the ways that you initially expect . . . but they will come. Keep asking to be shown your sign from the divine and also ask to remain open to noticing its arrival. Be sure to always give thanks when you notice a sign arrive to you and be in awe of how this magical connectedness works.

Linked Hearts

Our hearts are linked to those we've loved and lost.
It's a link to our ancestors that have come before us.
One that connects our spirit to the divine,
to the Universe, our Creator, to our angels.
That link is an Unbreakable chain, one that can withstand even heartbreak, darkness, and great loss.
It can become an even more powerful bond than the bond you knew before death arrived for them.
Love remains Now, Forever, Always.

MY HOPE

My hope in writing this handbook is to spread the truth about continued consciousness beyond bodily death and the ability that we have as grievers to maintain and even grow our connective bonds of love with those that we have lost but treasure most.

We have not lost our loved ones to death outside of the expiration of their physical body. In order to be witnesses to this truth, we simply have to learn their new language of energy. It is a language that communicates with vibration and frequency and that which we define as spirit or soul.

When we are no longer driving in human form, we are able to be all and in everything infinite. We can be in one place or a thousand places at one time. We end up being free of any boundary and wholly one with Creation itself. Our essence can in part remain with those whom we treasure most of all, and our relationships will forever be available for us to learn how to foster.

The ways in which we connect with those in spirit will be unique to all of us, and it needs to be witnessed and developed for oneself. Be genuine in belief of what is possible and then be consistent with your practice. We must not force but instead be open to releasing our hold and our desire to control our outcomes. We must trust in the Universe to unfold its truths and allow us to witness its magic-like occurrences. Then, we must pay attention... The signs will come.

Tomorrow

Tomorrow is not lost
Don't toss moments away
Live life for Now
Rejoice, Laugh, Explore, Play
Breathe in the air
Pause just to smile
Sit still and just be with yourself for awhile
Don't rush through time quickly
Embrace a slower pace
Living in the Now is never a race

www.ingramcontent.com/pod-product-compliance
Lightning Source LLC
LaVergne TN
LVHW011844060526
838200LV00054B/4161